# The Complete Book of
# BLACKJACK

# The Complete Book of
# BLACKJACK

◆

## A COMPREHENSIVE GUIDE
## TO WINNING STRATEGIES

### T. J. Reynolds

A LYLE STUART BOOK
Published by Carol Publishing Group

A Lyle Stuart Book
Published by Carol Publishing Group
Lyle Stuart is a registered trademark of Carol Communications, Inc.

Editorial, sales and distribution, and rights and permissions inquiries should be
addressed to Carol Publishing Group, 120 Enterprise Avenue, Secaucus, N.J. 07094.

In Canada: Canadian Manda Group, One Atlantic Avenue, Suite 105, Toronto, Ontario
M6K 3E7

Carol Publishing Group books may be purchased in bulk at special discounts for sales
promotion, fundraising, or educational purposes. Special editions can be created to
specifications. For details, contact Special Sales Department, Carol Publishing Group,
120 Enterprise Avenue, Secaucus, N.J. 07094.

Manufactured in the United States of America

10  9  8  7  6  5  4  3  2  1

Library of Congress Cataloging-in-Publication Data

Reynolds, T. J.
    The complete book of blackjack : a comprehensive guide to winning
strategies / T. J. Reynolds.
        p.  cm.
    Includes bibliographical references.
    ISBN 0–8184–0602-x (pbk.)
    1. Blackjack (Game)   I. Title.
GV1295.B55R44   1998
795.4'23—dc21                                                      97–44737
                                                                        CIP

*To my loving wife, Arja, for her patience
in enduring endless blackjack discussions over
the years, and her support and encouragement
regarding the completion of this text*

# CONTENTS

# PREFACE

"Another book on blackjack! Who needs it?"

This book is the result of researching, analyzing, testing theories, implementing various blackjack strategies, and playing the game for more than thirty-five years by the author. Still, with other blackjack books, videos, and computer games already available, how can this paperback offer any advantages?

Computer games are sometimes fun, but unfortunately they don't actually teach you much (although some do offer practice in card-counting). They are of limited value in the "real" world of casino play.

Many instructional videos are made for beginning and intermediate players. Although they usually cover the basics and a few additional topics, none is as completely comprehensive as this publication is. Also, the pace of a video is never precisely suited to any viewer. Videos are not portable, and therefore they are simply not as handy as a book can be.

Why this book rather than some other? Because every other blackjack book is now out of date, contains erroneous information, or was written to promote some new "wonder system"—whether or not it was practical to use under actual casino conditions. This volume, however, saves the reader valuable time, energy, and money, because it is an up-to-date overview of the entire world of blackjack. By accurately and concisely summarizing every bit of the significant blackjack literature currently available, this collation guides all players to achieve their own desired levels of expertise with virtually no financial risk.

Many blackjack books and theories (some originally written over thirty years ago) have survived various "revisions," but they are still of limited value to the modern player. Granted, a great debt is owed to a few pioneers who first studied the game systematically. But too many others have jumped onto the blackjack bandwagon for the wrong reasons.

Hoping to cash in on the demand of this rapidly growing market, assorted blackjack writers have scurried to publish questionable "theories" and offer new "systems" for sale. Invariably rife with inconsistencies and downright inaccuracies, these books offer up "facts" that are no longer true and contradictions that most beginning or intermediate players would likely not even notice. It is unfortunate that such practices are perpetuated.

The most prolific and misleading blackjack books on the market are those that profess to have the system that will make the reader rich— and certainly quicker, easier, and more efficiently than any other! These are primarily garbage. They tend to mislead readers by exaggerating possible gains, while underestimating the skill required. Also they tend to completely ignore the *considerable* risks involved. Let's be realistic here; the only people making money from these publications are their authors and publishers. Indeed, these books provide a disservice to students of the game by creating frustrating and hopeless situations, which this book avoids altogether.

This book was written for three reasons:

First, the explosive popularity of blackjack over the last decade, further encouraged by the ubiquitous "charity" and native peoples' casinos, has created a huge demand for reliable and impartial information about correct playing strategies and practical card-counting systems. At a fraction of the cost of outdated hardcovers, instructional videos, computer games, and the misleading and worthless blackjack "courses" that are available, this one little softcover provides everything the serious reader may ever wish to know about the game.

Second, even beginning players are now aware that blackjack is the only casino game that can be beaten in the long run. However, they are not sure which system best suits their individual needs. This publication properly instructs the novice, while carefully guiding more knowledgeable players toward achieving whatever level of expertise they wish to attain. Happily, the reader can be completely assured that there is no "filler" or "fluff" included within these pages. This book is meant to educate rather than entertain.

Third, it has always disturbed me to see greedy casinos take advantage of the innocent, hopeful players who have little or no grasp of basic blackjack "savvy" whatsoever. As a teacher, I have always been willing to share my knowledge and expertise with anyone truly interested in learning. By passing vital information on to the next generation of players via this book, my study and love of the game may never be lost.

No two blackjack players are alike. Nor does everyone learn in the same way. Depending upon your present level of commitment to the game, your desire to win, and the study time available, you can achieve your individual degree of expertise. If you fully utilize this book, your winning potential is unlimited. You can always study in more detail the many charts provided, reread the pages that cover your specific areas of weakness, or obtain additional publications recommended within if you are so inclined. In this way, you will always be able to take your play to higher and higher levels.

I have never been a good loser. "Show me a good loser and I'll show you a loser!" as the saying goes. I do not even consider myself a gambler in the usual sense of the word; for example, I've never bought a lottery ticket in my life. Rather, I consider myself a professional investor in the game. Blackjack can be a low-risk investment opportunity if played conservatively, and it offers more positive indications of a decent return on one's money than most business propositions. I only became interested in blackjack after Thorp's *Beat the Dealer* proved that a skilled player could emerge a winner over time. I hate losing money, but it irks me even more to see unscrupulous so-called blackjack experts boldly bilking naive players via expensive home study courses and/or their assorted harebrained advice.

Being a blackjack aficionado and a conscientious student of the game, I believe that I have read all of the worthwhile texts that are presently available on the subject. I am familiar with every known card-counting system—many of which cost me hundreds of dollars just to examine. The book you now hold in your hands began as some basic blackjack advice prepared for friends and family. Over the years it gradually took on a life of its own and ballooned into a synthesis of all the useful information gleaned from my successful playing experiences around the world and my in-depth study of the game.

I have learned and personally tested many card-counting programs, including the most highly touted blackjack systems available, and made thousands of tax-free dollars in the process. Formerly a fully licensed blackjack dealer myself, I rightfully boast a unique grasp of the game from both sides of the table. By carefully culling only the best advice to be included in this publication, I have saved you the onerous task of sifting through and properly evaluating the various tomes on your own. Having nothing to promote personally, I can assure you that this text is the most accurate, the most up-to-date, and the only unbiased one of its kind. Use it to learn how to play the game optimally, and consistent blackjack winnings will accompany you for the rest of your life.

To paraphrase Sir Isaac Newton: Only by standing upon the shoulders of giants can mere mortals expect to achieve greatness. I gratefully acknowledge the contributions of the true "giants" of blackjack, which have provided the basis for this publication. Without their insights and exhaustive efforts blackjack would still be just another game of chance. Blackjack has been very good to me; if I can share my expertise by returning something to future players of the game, then my main objective in researching and writing this paperback will have been realized.

T. J. Reynolds
March 1998

# The Complete Book of
# BLACKJACK

# GLOSSARY

| | |
|---|---|
| **H** | Hit |
| **S** | Stand |
| **D** | Double-down |
| **G** | Give up or Surrender |
| **P** | sPlit |
| **BS** | Basic Strategy |
| **MBS** | Modified Basic Strategy |
| **RC** | Running Count |
| **TC** | True Count |

# Introduction

Our local Lions Club sponsored an annual "Jamboree" in my village when I was a boy. It included several games of chance scattered around the perimeter of three or four midway rides. There was bingo and a few other carnival games, but they didn't appeal to me. I knew intuitively that winning at them was more a matter of luck than skill and that the odds were stacked against the player. One game, however, did attract my attention—a dice game called Over & Under.

Over & Under was played with two big wooden dice, which rolled down a ramp when the operator pulled up a trap. If you bet that their total would be over 7, or under 7, and you were right, you won even money. If you wagered correctly on their total being exactly 7, you were paid off 3 to 1. Allowable bets ranged from a quarter to $2.

While I was still too young to actually play Over & Under (the posted age requirement was sixteen), I happened upon a "foolproof" method of beating this game. Some of my older chums claimed to have made money at it, so I pried their "strategies" out of them.

"Just wait until two 'unders' come up in a row, and then bet on the 'over'—or vice versa," one guy suggested. "The law of averages is on your side that way!"

Another big winner (probably boasting a "killing" of $2 or $3 now that I recall it objectively) claimed that he just kept betting a quarter on "over" until he lost it; his next bet would be fifty cents. If he lost that one too, he would bet a dollar on the next roll, and so on. "You have to win eventually this way," he assured me. "You'd be pretty unlucky to lose four times in a row!"

Their advice seemed reasonable, so I decided that by combining these two winning strategies and adding a little twist of my own for insurance, I would really clean up at Over & Under—once I was old enough to play it!

The summer that I turned thirteen, I got a black leather jacket. I figured that I looked much older in it; after all, I was finally a teenager. With my collar turned up, the Over & Under operator that year allowed me to play without hesitation. What a thrill of anticipation I felt after placing my first wager. As I waited for those two dice to finally stop bouncing around, the real world suddenly turned into a slow-motion movie sequence. My heart was in my throat. I broke into a cold sweat and got wobbly in the knees. Even before I realized what total had come up, the attendant was giving me my first "free" quarter from his bulging money-pouch. I had won! Such a rush of excitement swept over me that I almost abandoned my playing strategy and laid down another quarter on the spot. I caught myself just in time.

My plan was this: Watch until three "overs" or "unders" came up in a row, then bet a quarter on the other one. Each time I won, I would wait for three more consecutive results, then bet a quarter on the opposite. When a loss resulted, I would watch until three-in-a-row happened again, then bet just another quarter on the other; therefore, when I won, I would get the quarter that I lost returned to me, and I would break even. However, if I lost that bet too, I would have to wait for three more somethings, then bet fifty cents, $1 and finally $2 if necessary. Using this betting method I would be completely safe for five successive losses. Surely it wouldn't come up four somethings in a row, for each of those five losses. To get wiped out completely on a final $2 wager, the "over" or "under" would have to come up eight straight times! Highly unlikely; so how could I possibly lose?

By the end of the evening I was up $2. Elated, I walked home scarcely touching the ground. I hadn't spent a cent elsewhere at the Jamboree that night, since I rarely ventured far from the Over & Under booth. But soon I began to feel guilty about taking the Lions Club's money; it was, after all, a charitable organization that helped the underprivileged! Suddenly, something my father once told me began to weigh heavily upon my conscience. "Never bet on a sure thing," he had cautioned me. "It's the same as stealing." Since I felt my "system" was invincible, in effect I had stolen the money! Instead of being proud of my achievement, I was ashamed of my behavior and didn't mention my feat to anyone. I resolved to lose the money back to the Over & Under operator the next night and forget about gambling forever.

Abandoning my "surefire" strategy completely, the next evening I played consecutive rolls of the dice with no regard to previous totals whatsoever, sometimes betting as much as $1 per roll—even laying out money on the 7 occasionally. To my amazement, in less than an hour I was up another $2! Later that evening, I spent my entire ill-gotten booty throwing darts at tickets for the Jamboree's grand prize drawing. I heaved a great sigh of relief as my wad of tickets fell into that drum; I had, in effect, finally succeeded in returning all the money I had won at Over & Under back into the Lions Club's coffers. But Lady Luck wasn't through toying with me that night. Likely due to my superabundance of tickets, I won the $25 "attendance prize" that was drawn later that evening.

This was my introduction to the vicissitudes of fortune. If things had gone the other way for me, as they more easily could have done, I might not have felt inclined to pursue any further forays into the world of gaming. I knew that having one of my tickets picked out of the hundreds of others in the drum was just a matter of turning the odds in my favor. Because of my initial success at Over & Under, however, I was captivated by the idea that perhaps "smart" players could, indeed, beat certain gambling games. I began wondering whether it might be possible, by means of intelligent playing (that is, completely understanding the odds involved and using them to one's advantage), to come out ahead in the long run.

What I didn't know at the time was that no betting system per se, regardless of its complexity, can ultimately win you money unless the odds are already in your favor. Similarly, other commonly misunderstood aspects mentioned in my personal anecdote related above—the psychology of gambling, probability theory, luck versus skill, etc.—are all carefully explained in the body of this book. I have purposely avoided including testimonials of specific successes or other such anecdotal comments in the following pages, because they prove nothing. Other texts are chock full of such "evidence," which is no more reliable than some woman in a soap commercial extolling the virtues of

XYZ detergent. Although they make more interesting reading than dry scientific research, I refuse to waste readers' time with such "facts." My primary purpose in this endeavor is to educate rather than to entertain.

Believe it or not, we are all gamblers in the strictest sense. Anyone who buys life, car, or fire insurance is gambling; these are all types of "proposition" bets. Have you ever played bingo? By walking across a busy street we put our lives at risk daily. In short, life itself is one big gamble. Don't let yourself feel too superior to the poor sap who becomes addicted to gambling—could you live without it in one form or another?

The reason I consider myself a nongambler is that I try to engage only in positive enterprises that possess a low level of risk. When I play roulette it is strictly for entertainment; I cannot rationally expect to emerge a winner in the long run. I am seldom interested in such games, because the bottom line is that one does not beat them in the end. As a businessman I prefer investing in real estate rather than the stock market. In good conscience I can rarely bring myself to continue playing financial "Russian roulette" regarding any investment, i.e., betting that I succeed against the odds.

I was always drawn to doing things my way, unconventional as it may have been. The idea of making money primarily by using my head intrigued me. Thanks to implementing my acquired knowledge and skills, I became financially independent and was able to retire comfortably before the age of forty. I'm not bragging; I worked hard, and I had some luck along the way too. The harder I worked, the "luckier" I became. In the intervening years I have lived a life of complete contentment. Before I get out of bed every morning I can think, "Well, what do I want to do today?" If this leisure-filled lifestyle appeals to you, read on; skillful blackjack playing can help make it happen for you too.

Not every reader will be as fortunate as I have been. Blackjack must not be viewed as "easy money" or a "get-rich-quick" scheme of any sort. On the first day of class one of my university professors stated, "Look at the person on your left and then look at the one on your right; only one of you three is apt to pass this course!" Apparently he had been reviewing the failure rates. As it turned out, this gloomy forecast proved quite accurate, but due primarily to his poor teaching rather than our learning abilities or desires to succeed. Unfortunately, I must make a similar prediction: Fewer than one-third of this book's readers will actually exert the necessary effort required to become expert blackjack players. The difference between me and my old professor, however, is that in the following pages I have made every effort to guide you to your desired level of achievement.

It is important to realize that if you are a traditional gambler, there is little need for you to read this book. If you simply enjoy playing games of chance—the exhilarating casino atmosphere, the free drinks, the social interaction, etc.—regardless of whether you walk out with more money than you had, the information presented herein must be considered truly peripheral. However, if you are more interested in making money from your casino visits, this book is your ultimate guide to success.

## Why Choose Blackjack?

The dice used in Over & Under and craps and the little white balls on roulette wheels all behave in a random fashion every time they roll. The numbers that they generate are totally independent of each other. Contrary to what many players believe, they bear no relationship to those numbers that may have come up in the past, assuming the games are run with completely "honest" equipment. (Gaffed wheels and loaded dice are always a possibility, but they are unlikely to be found in modern casinos. Management would be foolish to risk their gaming licenses on such things, especially since they would provide "hard" evidence that could be used against the house in court.)

According to the law of averages (although there is actually no such "law" in mathematics) if a certain number appears ten times in a row in roulette, it is just as likely as any other number to appear again the very next spin. Since there are usually thirty-eight possible slots on the wheel, the odds of any particular number coming up remain constant at once in every thirty-eight spins. Similarly, when playing craps, the probability of rolling a 12, for example, on your next toss is always one chance in thirty-six, even if those "boxcars" haven't appeared in the last hundred throws or more.

Bouncing balls, rolling dice, spinning wheels and the like—there is absolutely no way that these things can have a "memory" of previous results, in order to "even things out" eventually. Each specific number that they may produce at any given time can be predicted no more accurately than any other. Mathematically speaking, the odds in these games always remain constant in favor of the house. They are a "given" generated by truly "independent, random events." (See chapter 4 for details of probability theory.)

In roulette, craps, and every other casino game except blackjack, the odds remain constant, and *always* in favor of the house. No skill whatsoever is involved in playing; it's all a matter of luck on the player's part. Therefore, although you may win money at these games from time to time, they cannot and will not be beaten over the long run. (Poker can involve considerable playing knowledge and skills, but the house always takes its set percentage off the top of every pot.) Regardless of the skill level of other players at your table, or the different rules you may encounter, the fact remains that only blackjack can be beaten consistently over time.

Beating blackjack is accomplished by simply keeping track of which cards are brought into play, because at certain times during the game the odds actually favor the player. This process is known as "counting" and is much easier than most people assume. (Chapter 6 explains everything about counting.) Only by playing blackjack skillfully can you be guaranteed long-term winnings. This fact alone should be reason enough to choose blackjack as your casino game of preference. Everything you need to know in order to become an expert player is explained thoroughly herein.

"Why are you willing to give up a goose that lays golden eggs?" This is the recurring question skeptical students ask me regarding my writing of this text. Their doubts, in fact, are usually twofold: (1) Can blackjack actually be beaten? (2) If so, why would a successful player such as myself voluntarily part with this valuable knowledge?

1. If players can consistently win money from blackjack over time, how can the casinos afford to offer the game? The answer is, because only an extremely small number of people have acquired the knowledge necessary to beat the game, i.e., less than 2% of all players. Since *Beat the Dealer* first appeared in 1962, it has been well known that the game is vulnerable to card-counters. Worried casinos even tightened up their rules for this reason, but soon relaxed them again as their blackjack

business began to drop off. They quickly realized that so few players knew how to beat the game that they had nothing to fear. The casinos have continued to actually make *more* money from the game over intervening years because of the increased volume of players. Popularity surged primarily because practically everyone has been exposed to blackjack's positive publicity. The game can obviously be beaten; it's simply because so few players bother to learn how that modern casinos can make unprecedented earnings.

2. Blackjack has personally rewarded me greatly both financially and emotionally. Among other things, it has helped me live the good life much earlier than most. As a former teacher, I know the inner satisfaction that can be derived from sharing one's knowledge. Believe me, I am losing nothing by passing on the rather esoteric information in the following pages. In fact, I feel even richer for doing so. Writing this book has been essentially a labor of love for me. As a result of studying it, I hope, more players will force the greedy casinos to share a greater portion of their huge blackjack profits.

Even if you know absolutely nothing about the game, you now hold in your hands all that you will ever need in order to play at a professional level. The extent to which you make use of this text is entirely up to you. Its information can provide all the necessary strength and nourishment required, but you must eventually spring from your nest to try your own wings. Truly, only through your high-flying successes will my mentoring be complete.

# 1

# The Evolution

## "21"

The blackjack game we have grown to enjoy today was called simply "21" in North America until World War II began. John Scarne describes how the game became known as "Black Jack" in his *New Complete Guide to Gambling* (1961). According to Scarne, the horse-betting rooms around Evansville, Indiana, began offering payoffs of 3 to 2 whenever a player made a total of 21 on his first two cards. As a further enticement to play "21," if the first two cards consisted of the Ace and Jack of Spades (later Clubs were included, and eventually any suit), they offered a bonus payout of ten times the original bet. Soon, players began to call these two-card 21s "blackjacks" to distinguish them from their three-or-more-card 21s. By the end of the Second World War, casino blackjack was second in popularity only to the dice game known as craps, which persisted in being the leading form of recreational gambling into the mid-1960s. By the end of the 1970s, however, blackjack had surpassed all other casino games combined.

## Early Casino Advantages

The casinos didn't know their actual percentage advantage for blackjack even as late as 1930. Joe Treybal's *Handbook on Percentages,* published that year, is very vague (and inaccurate) about blackjack statistics. This is understandable, since practically every casino still had its own minor variations of the rules. Some did not require the dealer to hit a 16, while others ruled that even a "soft" 17 needed another card. Bonuses were paid on such hands as two 9s and three Aces, a 6, 7, and 8 of the same suit, three 7s, and seven-card 21s, to name only a few.

## Baldwin, Cantery, Maisel, and McDermott

In the early 1950s, four U.S. soldiers, Roger Baldwin, Wilbert Cantery, Herbert Maisel, and James McDermott, suggested that there was a definitive or "correct" way to play any hand of blackjack. After years of painstaking work using only simple desk calculators and mathematical principles, they published an article, "The Optimum Strategy in Blackjack," in September 1956. The article proved for the first time that "the player who mimics the dealer (drawing to 16 or less, standing on 17 or more, never doubling-down or splitting pairs) has an expectation of −0.056." This meant that the dealer had a 5.6% advantage. The article then proceeded to prove that by following certain basic strategy plays consistently, the average casino advantage over the player could be lowered to 0.32%. Without any regard to what cards had been played in the course of the game to that point, the Baldwin group presented for the first time a fairly accurate basic playing strategy that virtually allowed the player an even game. The systematic study of blackjack had begun.

## Edward O. Thorp

A professor at MIT, Edward O. Thorp, investigated the Baldwin group's work and subsequently wrote a computer program that allowed the composition of the remaining deck to be carefully analyzed as specific cards were removed during play. Thorp discovered that the player actually enjoyed a considerable advantage over the casino after certain cards were played and discarded. Thorp first published his findings in his famous *Beat the Dealer*, in 1962. Due to this book's tremendous popularity, a second edition quickly followed in 1966. Thorp's new basic strategy program was good enough to eliminate any house advantage whatsoever, providing a player advantage of 0.6%. By using this improved basic strategy along with any of several card-counting systems that Thorp developed, a blackjack player could at last have a significant edge in any single-deck game on the Las Vegas Strip. Blackjack would never be the same again.

## Julian Braun

Over the next ten years the correct basic playing strategy was refined by various mathematicians using powerful state-of-the-art computers. Most notably, Julian Braun, of IBM Corporation, wrote exhaustive programs that played every possible blackjack hand randomly against every possible dealer's up-card millions of times each. But even this wasn't good enough for Braun. He then proceeded to compare the effects of various rule changes on the outcome of particular hands. Tabulating his results, Braun was able to determine an accurate and truly definitive basic playing strategy, which could be varied slightly according to which set of rules one happened to be playing. He went on to devise charts for serious card-counters to memorize, which indicated how the basic playing strategies should be modified according to the specific composition of the deck(s) remaining to be dealt before the next shuffle. Braun's computer programming technology formed the basis of virtually all the counting systems that subsequently arose. He also wrote a simulation program that evaluated the performances of all major card-counting regimes, the results of which are reviewed in his book *How to Play Winning Blackjack* (1980). This text remains worthwhile reading even today.

## The Future of Blackjack

Thankfully, most casinos nowadays have adopted very similar rules. It is, therefore, a much easier job to determine the relative advantages of the assorted minor rule variations that still exist. Presently, the Vegas Club, located near the end of Fremont Street in downtown Las Vegas, boasts "The Most Liberal '21' Rules in the World." (See chapter 2 for details.)

Blackjack is still evolving today. It has changed considerably over the thirty-five years I have been acquainted with the game. Single-deck games are rare now, and none of the casinos offers the liberal rules that were once available. Double-deck games are still fairly common in Las Vegas, and their rules have remained quite unrestricted, but the floor people often tend to be paranoid about "counters." For example, I was once barred from the Barbary Coast casino after playing no more than twenty minutes at a double-deck $2 table. None of my bets had exceeded $10 and I had won less than $50 in all.

At the other extreme are the casinos that seem completely indifferent to counters. These are usually the ones using eight-deck shoes exclusively and/or high minimum betting limits—along with various restrictive rules. Cruise ships, however, are often oblivious to counters for different reasons altogether. (See chapter 5 for details.) The more decks used, the more tedious the counter's job tends to be. Higher minimums ensure that most players will be playing beyond their depth and will be more apt to experience "gambler's ruin" (explained in chapter 4).

Some skeptics predicted that the advent of the optimum basic strategy along with winning counting systems would inevitably spell doom for the game, i.e., the end of casino blackjack forever. Thorp's book, indeed, caused Las Vegas casinos to tighten up their blackjack rules drastically for a short time, but soon the rules were relaxed once more. After a few weeks, casino owners and managers realized that only a tiny percentage of players actually followed the correct new playing strategies that were widely available, and even fewer had learned to implement a viable counting system. It didn't make financial sense to alienate the whole blackjack-loving public just to protect themselves from an occasional card-counter. There is no doubt that it is more difficult for an unskilled player to win at blackjack today than it was before Thorp's publications appeared. However, truly dedicated students of the game will almost certainly continue to enjoy huge advantages for as long as the game is offered.

It is a safe bet that blackjack tables will remain permanent casino fixtures in the foreseeable future. As the popularity of the game continues to increase, the demand for even more tables will likely rise. The rules will necessarily stay fairly liberal or even improve, because as players become more knowledgeable they will demand more favorable odds. This economic reality has already become evident in the mid-1990s, as an increasing number of casinos have been pressured to offer more player-friendly options, such as surrender, single- and double-deck games, and lower table minimums. To protect themselves against counters, casinos may employ more shuffle machines, prohibit all midshoe entries, or take other "passive" measures (e.g., implementing only eight-deck shoes, or closing tables that are not full) that discourage counters but which do not alienate the regular hordes of unskilled players.

The arbitrary barring of knowledgeable players merely because they are suspected of counting cards may be ruled an illegal practice in the future. The late Ken Uston, successful blackjack team player and author of such books as *The Big Player* (1977), was the first to challenge in court a casino's right to refuse such skilled players continued access to the game. Sadly, Uston died before the issue was completely resolved. By barring counters the casinos are in effect saying, "Everyone has the right to lose money to us for any reason, but nobody has the right to win money due to an acquired skill." Initially, none of the casinos in Atlantic City could legally bar any player for possessing the skills necessary to count cards and to play the game in the most beneficial manner possible. Although this local statute was repealed in early 1979, the ethics of such a law remain in question.

# 2

# Modern Rules, Procedures, and Variations

Originally, the rules of blackjack were as varied as the individual casinos that first offered the game. Over the years, as players became more knowledgeable and demanded more consistent and favorable playing odds, the rules as outlined below became generally accepted. These have emerged as the most widely offered rules of the present day, but there are small casinos scattered throughout the world (and even in Las Vegas) that still adopt an assortment of old rules variations and "novelty-type" blackjack games.

Although blackjack is still evolving, virtually no significant rule changes have been applied to the basic game in many years. Some of the now rare and more peculiar playing variations still in existence are mentioned at the end of this chapter. These are included to inform the experienced player rather than to confuse the novice. In any case, it is of vital importance that the rules of whatever game you are playing be perfectly clear from the outset. There is little hope in succeeding at any game without first being entirely familiar with its rules. The skillful player may then use specific rules' variations to his advantage under certain circumstances, instead of being surprised or financially handicapped by them.

## The Most Common Blackjack Rules

### The Table

A typical blackjack table layout is shown below.

## Blackjack Table Layout

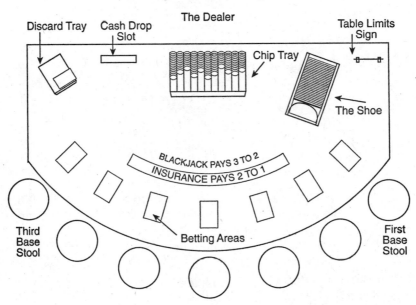

### The Cards

Standard poker-sized playing cards are used. Finding a game played with just one deck, however, is getting more difficult these days. Some casinos offer double-deck games, and you are usually better off to play there after familiarizing yourself with the "face-down" procedures that are normally used in single- and double-deck games. Six-deck games are by far the most common nowadays, although as many as eight decks are sometimes used.

The cards are shuffled and placed in a dealing device, known as a "shoe," from which the dealer delivers them to the players and himself as required. (No shoe is used in single- and double-deck games.) The first card out of the shoe is normally "burned," meaning that it is placed directly into the discard tray. (The colored plastic card-sized marker with which players cut the shuffled decks, and which the dealer then places a deck or two from the end of a shoe in order to indicate when to shuffle again, is often improperly referred to as a "burn card" as well. It is more correctly called simply a "shuffle card.")

*Card Values* A point value, or rank, is assigned to each card as follows: The different suits have no significance per se. 2s through 9s are counted at face value. 10s, Jacks, Queens, and Kings are worth 10 points each, and they are all called "10s" regardless of their apparent rank differences. The player may count any Ace as 1 point or 11 points, but the dealer must count an Ace as 11 in all "soft" hands totaling 17 or more. "Soft" hands are those that have at least one Ace that may be counted as 11 and still produce a total of 21 or less.

## Object of the Game

Blackjack is simply a contest between the dealer and yourself. Although up to six other players may play at your table simultaneously, each player competes individually against the dealer. The winner of each hand is determined by whose card total is higher—without being over 21 points. A "blackjack," sometimes called a "natural," consists of an Ace and any 10-valued card, only if these are the first two cards dealt in the hand. A blackjack is considered higher than any other hand even if the other hand totals 21 as well.

## Ties

If you tie the dealer with a total of 21 or less, you neither win nor lose your bet for that hand. This is called a "push," a term originating from the time when dealers actually pushed a player's wager back out of the betting area every time there was such a tie. Nowadays the dealer just "knocks" the table in front of a push to indicate that a payoff or loss was not merely overlooked.

## Wagering

The size of your bet must conform to the table's minimum and maximum limits. This range varies and is posted at each table. Some casinos allow "money plays," which are simply cash wagers placed inside the betting area, but normally cash must be exchanged for "chips" before a wager may be accepted. The playing chips are made of metal, clay, and/or plastic alloys, and they come in various denominations and colors, usually with the particular casino's logo on them. By convention, the red, green, and black chips are sold for $5, $25, and $100 respectively.

Before any cards are dealt, each player must decide upon the amount of the wager for the upcoming hand and place it in his/her designated betting area, known as the betting "box" or "spot." If several chips are being bet, they must be neatly stacked. Different denominations of chips being wagered in the same box must be arranged from the larger-valued ones on the bottom to the lesser-valued ones on top. Chips placed beside the betting area normally indicate to the dealer that the player wishes them "colored up" or "colored down," i.e., exchanged for chips of higher or lower value. A player may place a chip or two between the betting area and the dealer to indicate a separate bet is being made for the dealer in lieu of an outright tip: if the player's hand wins, the dealer wins the "toke" as well.

## The Deal

The shoe game begins in a clockwise direction, as the dealer gives each player at the table one card face up, thereby exposing its value. Then one card is dealt face down to the dealer, without being exposed to the players. This unseen card is known as the dealer's "hole" card, since there was an indentation in the early blackjack tables that accommodated it, thereby completely obscuring this card from the players' view. Each player then receives a second card face up, before the dealer places a face-up card on top of his hole card. A few casinos reverse the order in which the dealer receives his/her two cards, but most give the player as little time as possible to view the dealer's up-card before being required to make his first playing decision. In shoe games, the player is never allowed to touch his cards. Single- and double-deck games that are dealt face down necessarily require the player to handle the cards, but only with one hand at a time.

## Peeking

If the dealer's up-card is a 10-valued card or an Ace, in order to save time playing out all of the hands perhaps for naught, most casinos require the dealer to "peek," i.e., to carefully check the hole card immediately, being careful to allow no player to see its value. If the hole card provides the dealer with a blackjack and therefore an unbeatable total, the dealer exposes it at once and quickly collects all of the losing bets around the table in a counterclockwise direction. Of course, if you also have a blackjack, it is considered a push and you neither win nor lose the hand.

## Playing Decisions

After placing your bet and receiving your first two cards, you must then decide how to play your hand. This is where skill enters the game, since whether you win or lose depends largely upon what choices you make at this point. Considering the value of the dealer's up-card and your own starting pair, you must decide whether to take "insurance" if offered, "surrender," "split," "double," "hit" (and perhaps "bust" as a result), or "stand." These choices must be made for every hand you receive, in the order listed above. The playing decisions are explained below.

## Insurance

Whenever the dealer's up-card is an Ace, he will ask whether you wish to buy "insurance." The dealer asks this before peeking at the hole card. What he actually wants to know is, "Would you like to bet that I have a 10-valued card in the hole, thereby giving me a blackjack?"

Insurance is a completely separate side bet, which has nothing whatsoever to do with your hand. You only have to decide whether or not to wager that the hole card is, indeed, a 10-valued card. (A "true 10" is a 10 *only*, while a "10-valued card" is *any* face card *or* true 10 and is designated hereafter as "T.") Many beginning players feel that there is some relationship between the value of their first two cards and the advisability of the insurance option, i.e., that they should take insurance when holding a good hand but not necessarily when holding a poor starting total. Nothing could be further from the truth; in fact, in chapter 4 you will see that exactly the opposite is true. Unless you are a counter of cards, the insurance wager is completely unrelated to the cards you hold and is only concerned with whether or not the dealer's hole card is a T.

You make the insurance bet, if you wish, by placing an amount equal to one-half your current wager beside your original bet, in the area on the table layout designated "Insurance Pays 2 to 1." Many casinos allow you to insure for less than half your original wager, but never more, and usually exactly half is required. The dealer then peeks at the hole card. If it is a T, she has a blackjack and immediately takes your original losing bet (unless you also have a blackjack) or pays off your winning insurance bet 2 to 1. Therefore, if you take the insurance bet and win, you break even on the hand overall. If the dealer does not have a T in the hole, you lose your insurance bet, because you were betting that the dealer would get a blackjack, and this was not the case. You then continue normal play with your original hand versus the dealer's Ace up-card, even though you lost the insurance wager. When you do not wish to make the insurance wager, simply do not push out any chips into the insurance area of the layout.

If you are holding a blackjack when the dealer asks, "Insurance, anyone?" you may decide to insure it by taking what is known as "even money," i.e., an amount exactly equal to your wager, instead of chancing the 3 to 2 payout for your blackjack, if the dealer's hole card happens not to be a T. If the dealer does have a blackjack, then you would get nothing without the insurance bet, since the result would be a push. An even-money payoff before the dealer checks to see if he also has a blackjack is a sure-win situation, but you are giving up the potential 3-to-2 payoff that a blackjack would normally provide.

Taking even money for a blackjack is exactly equivalent to taking insurance. If you insure your blackjack and the dealer does have a 10-valued card in the hole (i.e., a 10, J, Q, K), then you gain the same amount as your original bet, since you win twice the half-bet wagered on the insurance and push with your blackjack. If the dealer does not get the blackjack, then you are still up an amount equal to your original bet, since you get paid 3 to 2 for your blackjack, while losing the half-bet you wagered on the insurance. Either way, you are always up "even money" when insuring a blackjack.

## Surrender

The concept of "surrender" was introduced in 1958 by the Continental Casino in Manila. After the dealer determined that he did not have a blackjack, a player could throw in his hand after any number of cards, as long as he hadn't busted, and he would lose only half of his original wager.

In 1978, Resorts International in Atlantic City offered players the surrender option on any first two cards, *before* the dealer checked for blackjack. This became known as "early" surrender, and the 1958 variation as "late" surrender. Although very popular and profitable for all knowledgeable players, early surrender was discontinued after only a short trial period and has not been offered anywhere since. Late surrender, which is now common in Las Vegas, Atlantic City, and other centers around the world, now consists of giving up your hand and half of your bet upon viewing your first two cards. As in the original rule, surrendering is permitted only if the dealer has no blackjack.

Another rare variation of surrender that still exists in a few foreign casinos is called "five-card surrender." If the player succeeds in drawing five cards without busting, he may relinquish his hand and receive back his original wager plus one-half of it. In this case the player is guaranteed a "half-win" while giving up the possibility of a "full win." (For correct basic strategy plays concerning this uncommon rule, see Braun's *How to Play Winning Blackjack*, [1980], pages 71-72.)

After viewing your first two cards and the dealer's up-card, you may figure that you have little chance of winning your hand. At this point many casinos now offer the late surrender option, which allows you to give up your hand, while losing only half of your bet, after the dealer peeks and determines that he has no blackjack. In a shoe game, you indicate your intention to surrender by simply saying aloud, "I surrender." This is the only instruction that must be given verbally to a dealer. In single- or double-deck games that are dealt face down, tossing your two cards face up onto the table toward the dealer is normally all that is required to tell the dealer that you wish to surrender.

## Splitting

If your first two cards happen to have the same point value, you may decide to split them up, thereby creating two separate hands. You indicate your desire to split by sliding equal-value chips up beside the current wager in your betting area. The dealer will then automatically move the cards apart and deal you another card on each split hand. If one of these "second" cards happens to have the same point value as the first two, you can usually resplit, creating a maximum of up to four distinct hands, each one necessarily being matched with an equivalent initial wager. The number of times that you may resplit varies with individual casinos. You are normally allowed to split Aces only once, however, and resultant blackjacks are then deemed to be only 21s. If these hands are eventual winners, they are paid off with only even money instead of the 3-to-2 ratio that true blackjacks would warrant.

## Doubling

Considering your initial two-card point total, you may figure that you have a good chance of beating the dealer's final total, even if you draw only one more card. In this case you may double the wager of the hand by sliding equal-value chips up behind the original bet in your box. When you double your bet in this way you must take just one additional card to complete your hand. This is called "doubling-down," or simply "doubling," since you are actually doubling your wager on that particular hand. The dealer usually acknowledges the double by placing your final card sideways.

## Hitting

When your first two cards add up to 8 or less, or if you receive a "stiff" hand, i.e., one that totals 12 to 16 points, you may desire another card to try to improve your total. Indicate this to the dealer by scratching a finger on the table behind your cards or by distinctly pointing to them. The dealer will then give you the next card out of the shoe. This process is called "hitting." You may keep on taking hits until you are satisfied with your total or until you "bust."

## Busting

You "bust" or "break" when your card total goes over 21 points, in which case the dealer immediately picks up your wager, and then your cards. The dealer busts when his total exceeds 21 as well, but by that time your bet is already lost. In this case a tie is not considered a push, even though you may have broken the 21-point limit with exactly the same total as the dealer.

## Standing

If your first two cards give you a "pat" hand, i.e., one that totals 17 or more and contains no Aces being counted as 11, you may be content with it, and decide to draw no more cards. This is called "standing." You indicate this choice by waving a hand horizontally over your cards. Hand signals are very important, because in a noisy casino (or if the dealer speaks a foreign language) verbal instructions are too easily misunderstood. In fact, they are usually not accepted. Hand signals are de rigueur in most casinos, since they can be verified if necessary by the overhead video cameras that are normally concealed in the ceilings, in case any dispute arises that cannot be settled satisfactorily by the pit boss.

## Back-playing

When the tables are very crowded, some casinos allow players standing behind the seated players to place bets in the same boxes, just behind the original wagers. The seated player must always consent to this arrangement, and the "outside" player is forced to abide by any playing decisions made by the seated player. However, if the seated player proceeds to split or double-down, the outside player may match his original bet accordingly, or simply abide by the results of the first hand of the split. When the first split hand is doubled by the seated player, the outside player may decide to double as well or simply stand with the total obtained by the additional card. Allowing outside players to play in seated players' boxes can create confusing situations, e.g., when only one player takes insurance; therefore, most casinos avoid these potential problems by simply opening up additional tables whenever conditions warrant them.

## Disputes

If your hand signal to hit or to stand is not distinct enough, the dealer may inadvertently give you an unwanted card or pass you by without your desired hit. In such an instance, or when any other dispute arises, the pit boss will be called over by the dealer in order to mediate a resolution. If this does not satisfy the player, the pit boss may choose to make a final decision by examining the videotape from the table's "eye in the sky." This is actually done very infrequently. In the thirty-odd years that I have been observing the game, a resolution "from above" has been necessary only once. If there is genuine doubt and the wager is small, pit bosses tend to side with the player in order to foster good public relations. "The eye" is the casino's main surveillance technique and is employed primarily for security reasons. In any case, the decision of the pit boss is final regarding the settlement of various playing controversies.

## Resolution

After all of the players in turn from the dealer's left have chosen to stand on their totals or have busted, the dealer turns over her hole card, then draws additional cards, as necessary, until she gets a pat hand or busts. Some casinos do not consider a soft 17 to be a pat hand for their dealers and insist that they must hit this total. (Again, "soft" totals are those obtained when at least one Ace is counted as 11 points, instead of only 1.) Others require the dealer to stand on all 17s or more. Usually, this rule is printed upon the table layout itself.

Once a dealer achieves a pat hand, she must stop drawing cards. If your final total is higher, the dealer will proceed to pay you an amount equal to the bet(s) in your betting area. A blackjack will gain you your original wager plus half as much again. Of course, you lose all the chips in your box whenever your total is lower than the dealer's. When the dealer breaks, however, all players remaining in the hand win with their hands regardless of their totals. It is customary for dealers to award blackjack holders their 3-to-2 payoffs immediately upon determining that the dealer does not also have a blackjack, rather than waiting to pay off these naturals in the usual counterclockwise manner.

For visually oriented readers, the following flowchart may better illustrate the sequence of events, the choices you have, and the decisions you must make in order to resolve every hand of blackjack.

# PLAYING DECISIONS

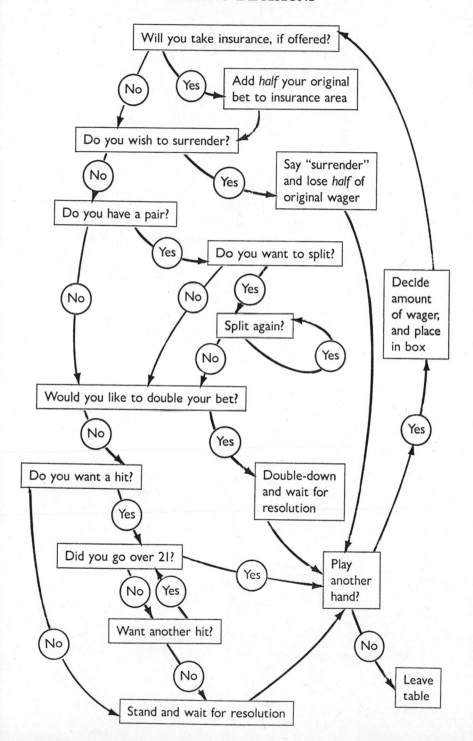

## Rule Variations

The general rules and procedures of blackjack mentioned above are adopted globally. There are, however, some exceptions that should be noted.

A few casinos still do not allow you to double-down after splitting a hand, but the trend is definitely toward the more liberal rule application. This is an important factor to consider when deciding whether or not to split low pairs. Some casinos do not permit soft doubling, i.e., doubling-down when an Ace is one of your first two cards. Still others allow doubling on two-card totals of 10 and 11 only. All casinos in Atlantic City have identical rules, but elsewhere it is advisable to check out individual casino rule variations before deciding to play seriously. These variations are covered in subsequent chapters, since such adverse playing conditions do have an impact upon the strategy you should use in resolving certain hands properly.

### The Vegas Club

A small downtown Las Vegas casino called the Vegas Club claims to have "The Most Liberal '21' Rules in the World." There you can double-down after any two, three, or four cards, resplit Aces, and keep splitting any other pair as many times as you wish. If you draw six cards totaling 21 or less, you are an automatic winner regardless of what total the dealer achieves. The table betting limits are $3 to $500 for each hand. Vegas Club also offers the surrender option.

The obvious question arises, "Why would anyone play anywhere *else* if given the choice?" The Vegas Club has only six-deck shoe games in which dealers are required to hit soft 17s. Vegas Club dealers use two discard trays to hold the used cards while waiting for the shuffle card to appear, a practice designed to discourage counters who "track" shuffles (see tip #94, page 199). Also, the shuffle card is placed almost halfway up the shoe, and since this casino employs no shuffle machines, you waste a lot of time watching the dealers shuffle.

### "Charity" Casinos

These attractions, which are becoming more popular every year, are usually held in local hotels or clubs under the auspices of a legitimate charity sponsor. Although a portion of charity casino winnings does go to the advertised charity (sometimes as high as 50 percent of the profits), you may wish to donate directly to these organizations rather than trying to make money from their blackjack games. Beware of certain tables whose rules are extremely bad; for example, sometimes all pushes lose to the dealer, or blackjacks pay only even money. Patronize these "fly-by-night" casinos and other "Vegas Night" galas only for the fun of it or to gain more playing confidence. They are good places to get real blackjack-playing experience without the risk of losing a lot of money quickly, since their table minimums are often as low as $1 a hand. But since the table maximum can be as low as $10, don't expect to make much money at such events. Besides, for some people it simply doesn't feel right to walk away with cash that the local charity needs— and was hoping to win from unsuspecting sponsors like yourself.

## Europe

In most European casinos, as in many local charity casinos, the dealer does not draw a second card (normally the unseen hole card) until after all players have completed their hands. So, if you were to double or split against an Ace or T, and the dealer eventually ended up with a blackjack, you would lose your original bet, plus your double and/or split wager as well. At the few Las Vegas casinos and others around the world that do not peek for blackjacks, only the player's original wager is lost if the dealer winds up with a blackjack.

## Dealing Down

One rule variation with which everyone should be familiar was mentioned in passing above and occurs mainly in single- or double-deck games. It is known as "dealing down." In shoe games, you receive all of your cards face up and are never allowed to touch them. But when the dealer is able to hold in his hand all of the cards used, your first two cards are normally dealt face down. You then must pick them up, using only one hand. You ask for a hit by lightly brushing them toward you upon the table's surface. If you decide to surrender, or you bust, then you are expected to toss your cards face up toward the dealer. When you want to stand, you indicate this choice by sliding your initial two cards face down under your wager. Double-down by pushing out an equal value of chips behind your original bet inside the betting box, then tuck your cards underneath it, still face down. You will receive your additional card face down and may examine it if curiosity gets the better of you, but normally it is left for the dealer to flip over when resolving the hand. Split by spreading your pair face up and putting equivalent chips up behind the second card, thereby making two separate hands.

The rules at tables that are dealt down are usually slightly more restrictive than those for adjacent shoe games even in the same casino. It is common to disallow doubling after splitting. You may find that surrender is not permitted in single- or double-deck games, even if it is allowed elsewhere throughout the casino. Table limits are usually higher as well, so it behooves the card-counting player to consider the disadvantages along with the benefits to be derived from playing in down games.

## Mid-Shoe Entry

Entering a game of blackjack is generally as simple as finding an open spot at a table and placing a bet in the appropriate area. After resolving the hand in progress, the dealer usually accepts any newcomer into the game for the next hand immediately. Increasingly, however, casinos are demanding that players enter the game only after a shuffle. Similarly, if a seated player decides not to play a hand, he may not be permitted to reenter the game until after the next shuffle is completed. Disallowing such midshoe entries is a practice more common in Atlantic City than Las Vegas at present but may be found almost anywhere. Casino managers believe that counters are thwarted by this measure, but for the facts see chapter 6. By adopting proper wagering practices, counters are unaffected—except that "Wonging" (see tip #37, page 187) is no longer possible.

## Wagering Variations

### Table Limits

The range of minimum and maximum bets can vary greatly within the same casino but is usually clearly posted at each table. One-dollar minimum tables are increasingly hard to find nowadays, while $25 minimums are getting more common, especially in the newer Canadian casinos. The range between minimum and maximum bets is generally much greater in Las Vegas casinos than in smaller casinos such as those found in the Bahamas, the Caribbean, cruise ships, or charity games. Many casinos require players playing more than one spot to wager at least twice the table minimum in each box.

## Over and Under

The Atlantis Casino on Paradise Island, Nassau, and the Flamingo in Laughlin, Nevada (among others), offer a blackjack side-bet variation, known as the "over and under 13" proposition. According to the total of the player's first two cards, even money is paid if he bets correctly. For this wager, Aces are counted as 1s only. A total of exactly 13 is a loser, since it is neither over nor under 13. See chapter 4 for more details about this unusual side-bet variation.

## Exposed Hole Card

Bob Stupak's Vegas World casino in Las Vegas introduced a blackjack variation known as "Double Exposure," which can still be found from time to time in various modified forms. Both dealer's cards are dealt face-up. No soft doubling is allowed. Pairs may be split only once. Players win blackjack ties but lose all other ties. A blackjack comprised of the Jack and Ace of Spades pays double, and so does arriving at 21 with the 6, 7, and 8 of any one same suit; normal blackjacks pay only even money. Stupak went bankrupt, but certainly not because of this game. Vegas World is no longer in existence. The landmark casino that Stupak built in Vegas is now known as the Stratosphere Tower. At 135 stories, it remains the tallest structure in the United States west of the Mississippi.

## Multiple-action

During the mid-1990s the Tropicana casino in Atlantic City introduced a slight twist to the regular game of blackjack by allowing a player to make up to three separate wagers on an upcoming hand. The dealer starts with the same up-card against the three consecutive player bets. The player keeps the same cards versus all three dealer's hands. The hands are played out in the usual manner, and if a player goes bust, all three bets are lost. Splitting, doubling, and insurance are permitted on any or all of the original hands. No surrendering is allowed in multiple-action blackjack, but otherwise the rules are comparable to the normal game. For counters this game offers some significant advantages (see tip #86, page 197 for details).

## Equipment and Procedures

### Shuffling Procedures

When I first visited Las Vegas, in 1968, there were single-deck games that were dealt down to the last card before the dealer would reshuffle. How times have changed! Now even double decks have shuffle cards inserted at a half-deck to a full deck from the bottom. Now six-deck shoes with their shuffle cards placed about one deck from the end are by far the most common in Vegas and throughout the world. Shuffling machines that can handle up to eight decks are widespread and speed up the game, but they have made "clump" tracking (see tip #94, page 199) impossible for counters.

In Walter Nolan's *The Facts of Blackjack* (1984), the "Bart Carter Shuffle" is mentioned as one of the ways a casino can negate the effect of counting. After about a deck of cards has been dealt from the shoe, those cards are shuffled and split into three separate stacks. These stacks are then inserted, at specified intervals, back into the remaining cards in the shoe. This variant reshuffling procedure allows cards already brought into play to appear in subsequent play, together with cards that are appearing for the first time from the shoe. The dealer has more opportunity to cheat when using the Carter shuffle, but players dislike it mainly because it interrupts the flow of the game. It simply looks too suspicious and consequently is used rarely nowadays.

### Dual Discard Trays

There is no need for alarm if you notice some casinos using two discard trays. This practice was originally intended to thwart counters who practiced clump tracking and is still quite successful in that regard. In gathering up used cards, the dealer alternates placing them in one discard tray and then the other. The casino's explanation for using two trays is that with six- and eight-deck shoes, a single pile of discards tends to topple over too easily. Dual discard trays do not significantly affect any counting system whatsoever. The ease with which a counter determines the TC (true count) is disturbed a little, but not by much.

## "No-Peek" Devices

In order to increase the pace of the game, many casinos that do not allow dealers to personally peek for blackjacks when they have a T or Ace showing have installed small electronic devices into the tables in front of the dealers. These little "eyes" scan the hole card and up-card simultaneously. Whenever a T or Ace happens to be the dealer's up-card, he simply slides the card into this gadget. If a T-Ace combination exists, a small red light comes on, indicating that the hand is over. If no blackjack is present, a green light allows the hand to proceed normally. Where no such devices exist, or where dealers are not allowed to peek at their hole cards when a potential blackjack is imminent, the time taken to play out each player's hand is wasted whenever the dealer ends up with a blackjack. The no-peek device is simply a safeguard, designed to protect the casino from possible dealer-player collusion, while at the same time permitting play to continue in the most efficient manner possible. It also challenges card-counters to immediately tally up all of the cards on the table before the dealer quickly scoops them away whenever a red light indicates a dealer blackjack.

## Special Variations

### Spanish 21

Perhaps the most reprehensible, if not truly heinous, variation of the game that has been foisted upon the unsuspecting blackjack public recently is the game billed by the Vegas Strip and downtown casinos alike as Spanish 21. The Lady Luck on Fremont Street even has the audacity to advertise "Over 99% Payback" for this blackjack look-alike.

For Spanish 21 games, all the usual blackjack rules and procedures apply, but in addition:

1. A player's blackjack always beats the dealer's blackjack and is paid off with the usual 3-to-2 bonus.

2. A player's total of 21 is always a winner and is paid off immediately, even if the dealer also ends up with a 21; i.e., no pushing here as is normally done.

3. Players may split any cards of equal value (including Aces), creating as many as four separate hands from the original one. Furthermore, hitting and doubling on such split hands is also allowed.

4. Players may double their bet and take just one more card any time they wish, i.e., after 2, 3, 4, or more cards—even after splitting.

5. After doubling, a player who is not satisfied with the final draw of the hand may take back the doubled portion and surrender, thereby losing only the original portion of the wager. This variation of surrender is called the "double-down rescue."

6. Both the surrendering and insurance options of normal blackjack continue to be permitted in this game.

As if these half-dozen very liberal rule changes were not enough, the Spanish 21 player receives *bonus* payoffs for certain hands as follows:

1. A total of 21 comprised of five, six, or seven separate cards pays a bonus at the rate of 3 to 2, 2 to 1, and 3 to 1 respectively. A 21 with more than seven cards pays 3 to 1.

2. A 21 consisting of a 6, 7, and 8, is paid a bonus of 3 to 2, 2 to 1, or 3 to 1 depending upon whether the cards are of mixed suit, all the same suit, or all Spades respectively.

3. If your initial hand consists of three 7s, this rare 21 is rewarded with a bonus of 3 to 2, 2 to 1, or 3 to 1 depending upon whether the 7s are of mixed suit, all the same suit, or all Spades respectively.

4. Most casinos that offer Spanish 21 also offer an additional bonus for players who receive three 7s of the same suit whenever the dealer's up-card is also a 7. If the player has bet a minimum of $25 on the hand, he gets paid the super bonus of $5,000, and all other players at the table get what is known as an "envy" bonus of $50 each. If only $5 is wagered on the hand, however, the super bonus is reduced to $1,000, and no envy bonuses are paid.

If at first glance Spanish 21 blackjack seems too good to be true, it's because it is. The only obviously disadvantageous rules for the player are that the game is played from six-deck shoes only and that the dealer is required to hit all soft 17s. These restrictions are quite common and in themselves offer no real deterrent. Why this game is so deadly for the novice blackjack player is explained under tip 84 (see page 197).

## "No-house" Blackjack

This variation of blackjack is commonly played at home. There is no fixed "house" to benefit from the different rules, because the dealer is continually changing. Typical rule variations: Dealer wins all pushes; blackjacks pay 2 to 1, but there is no insurance offered; splitting and doubling are allowed, but only one card on split Aces; any five-card hand under 21 is an automatic winner.

Custom normally dictates that whenever you get a blackjack, you become the dealer. If the dealer gets blackjack, she keeps the deal. If both dealer and player draw blackjacks, the dealer maintains the deal. When two or more players receive blackjacks, the holder of the natural that is dealt first gets to be the next dealer. If any player does not wish to be the dealer (because of low funds, or whatever the reason), he can offer to sell the deal to the highest bidder among the other players.

No-house blackjack is increasing in popularity and is legal in parts of Canada and the United States as long as the shoe is passed around in such a manner that there is no fixed house.

## Tournaments

Annual full-fledged blackjack tournaments that involve a thousand or more players competing for prizes of $50,000 and up are not uncommon in Las Vegas. More popular, however, are the numerous mini-tournaments that are held daily. Practically every large casino now hosts these scaled-down attractions, which appeal to novice blackjack players and seasoned veterans alike. A typical buy-in of $25 can put anyone in contention for a $500 first prize and perhaps one of three $100 consolation prizes.

Mini-tournaments are generally run as follows. Each registered player receives $1,000 worth of "tournament" chips and can wager from $10 to $1,000 per hand. All the usual blackjack rules apply, except that a button is passed around the table clockwise in order to indicate where the dealer starts dealing each hand. Unlike real blackjack, however, players compete against each other to determine a table winner after a set period of time, normally half an hour. After time expires, three final hands are dealt to all remaining players at the table who still have chips to wager. Once these hands are resolved, the player who has accumulated the most value in tournament chips wins the round and then proceeds to the next table, where he receives a fresh stack of $1,000 chips to play against five or six other table winners. It usually takes three such rounds to establish an overall champion, with all players who reach the final table winning at least their entry fees back.

While blackjack tournaments and mini-tournaments are obviously great fun, the main problem is that chance rather than skill usually determines who ends up with the prize money. Second, while the odds of winning are certainly better than with, say, keno, the potential return on your entry fee is not great. Professional players know that winning blackjack is a slow process; in just a couple of hours anything can happen and normally does. This is not enough time to differentiate a knowledgeable player from a merely lucky one. While counters do have an obvious advantage over beginning players, who wins a table (or tournament) is almost always decided upon the last hand (or two) dealt, proper blackjack playing strategy being tossed out the window. Wagering assumes an unnatural significance. Since it is necessary to win more than all other opponents, tournament players are forced to make ridiculous plays such as doubling down on pat hands or even blackjacks.

"Rapid blackjack," a variation of tournament blackjack, is simply a shortened mini-tournament, usually lasting only one shoe plus three hands.

This page is left intentionally blank so that you can tear out the chart on the back of the page and use it at a card table. (If the idea of tearing up a book offends you, you can always photocopy it.)

# The Basic Strategy (BS) Chart

## The DEALER is showing a:

| YOU have: | 2 | 3 | 4 | 5 | 6 | 7 | 8 | 9 | T | A |
|---|---|---|---|---|---|---|---|---|---|---|
| 5–8 | H | H | H | H | H | H | H | H | H | H |
| | | | | | | | | | | |
| 9 | H | D | D | D | D | H | H | H | H | H |
| 10 | D | D | D | D | D | D | D | D | H | H |
| 11 | D | D | D | D | D | D | D | D | D | H |
| | | | | | | | | | | |
| 12 | H | H | S | S | S | H | H | H | H | H |
| 13 or 14 | S | S | S | S | S | H | H | H | H | H |
| 15 | S | S | S | S | S | H | H | H | G | H |
| 16 (not 8s) | S | S | S | S | S | H | H | G | G | G |
| | | | | | | | | | | |
| 17–21 | S | S | S | S | S | S | S | S | S | S |
| 17 (soft)* | H | H | H | H | H | H | H | H | H | H |
| 18 (soft)* | S | S | S | S | S | S | S | H | H | H |
| | | | | | | | | | | |
| A, 2 or A, 3 | H | H | H | D | D | H | H | H | H | H |
| A, 4 or A, 5 | H | H | D | D | D | H | H | H | H | H |
| A, 6 | H | D | D | D | D | H | H | H | H | H |
| A, 7 | S | D | D | D | D | S | S | H | H | H |
| A, 8 or A, 9 | S | S | S | S | S | S | S | S | S | S |
| | | | | | | | | | | |
| 2, 2 or 3, 3 | P | P | P | P | P | P | H | H | H | H |
| 4, 4 | H | H | H | P | P | H | H | H | H | H |
| 6, 6 | P | P | P | P | P | H | H | H | H | H |
| 7, 7 | P | P | P | P | P | P | H | H | H | H |
| 8, 8 | P | P | P | P | P | P | P | P | P | P |
| 9, 9 | P | P | P | P | P | S | P | P | S | S |
| A, A | P | P | P | P | P | P | P | P | P | P |

H = Hit   S = Stand   P = sPlit   D = Double-Down
G = Give up (i.e., surrender if allowed, otherwise hit)

1. Never take insurance.
2. Never split 5s or T's.
* Always hit soft hands totalling 17 or less, whenever doubling-down is not an option. Notice that A,7 is a soft 18, but one with doubling potential. Stand with soft 19s and 20s against any dealer up-card.

# 3

# The Basic Strategy

If you learn only one thing from this book, the proper basic strategy (BS) is definitely what it should be. Knowing how to play every possible hand with the odds in your favor is unquestionably the single most important skill for any player to master. This ability alone allows you to at least break even, whenever you play the game, practically anywhere in the world. Do yourself this huge favor: Memorize the BS so that you can play blackjack for the rest of your life without worrying about handing over any of your hard-earned cash to the casinos unnecessarily. Whenever you do lose a hand, or even an entire session, just knowing that you played it 100% properly will help ease your frustration. There are few worse feelings in blackjack than those that surface after losing hands you suspect you may have played incorrectly, simply because you were unsure of the best thing to do. This chapter can eliminate those gnawing doubts forever.

Unfortunately, BS takes a few hours of study to master. It is the hardest single thing you will learn about blackjack. More difficult than counting, or any other aspect of the game, BS is nevertheless the foundation of all professional play.

## The Importance of BS

The good news is that the following BS chart is the only one you will ever need to learn in order to win consistently. It shows the absolute best, mathematically proven, correct play for every possible two-card player total versus all possible dealer up-cards, for every shoe game you will ever encounter. These recommended plays are not merely my opinions; they are indisputable. High-speed computers have played out each hand variation randomly millions of times, substantiating the data presented. Understanding this chart, and following it faithfully, can give you an edge (even without the use of any counting system) over all but the most greedy casinos, whose very restrictive rules may still afford them a minuscule advantage.

Other books offer page after page of virtually incomprehensible tables, enough to overwhelm even the most determined individual. However, most of their chart variations involve very minor BS adjustments, depending upon dozens of various rule possibilities: for example, whether you are allowed to double-down after splitting; whether you are playing in a single- or double-deck game, as opposed to a shoe; whether surrender is offered; whether the dealer hits soft 17s; or perhaps (as in most casinos outside North America, or local charity games), whether the dealer is required to take a hole card. Confronted with this multitude of mind-boggling charts and tables, an ordinary player can easily become frustrated, and perhaps give up learning any BS whatsoever!

Rest assured that the single chart below is, truly, all you will ever need to know to keep from losing money at blackjack in any casino where reasonably favorable rules apply. Abiding by this 100% correct BS table enables you to win more when you have strong beginning totals and, therefore, an advantage over the house. It also ensures that you will lose less when you draw weak initial cards and the dealer has the advantage. After all, saving money in bad situations is just about as important as winning it in the good ones. Keep in mind that this basic strategy (BS) indicates the definitive, optimum way to play every hand that you can possibly receive, assuming that you have not been tracking (counting) the cards, using one of the systems presented in chapter 6.

The only bad news regarding BS study is that it does take

considerable effort to absorb well enough to employ flawlessly under actual casino conditions. Although learning most of the proper BS plays will obviously tend to improve your game, it is absolutely essential that you know all of the correct plays and follow them relentlessly in order to eliminate the casinos' advantage. Misplaying as few as one hand in twenty is providing more than enough margin of error to allow them to maintain an insurmountable edge. Also, if you ever hope to win significant amounts of money playing blackjack in the future by learning additional skills such as those presented in later chapters of this book, becoming completely familiar with BS is your initial foundation step. In short, mastering BS is essential for all aspiring long-term winners. Take the time to absorb BS in its entirety now. It is of paramount importance that BS be thoroughly digested and incorporated into your daily play. Forget about hunches, intuition, or "gut feelings" and merely follow BS precisely and consistently. Without knowing something about the composition of the remaining cards to be dealt, BS is always your best course of action. Learn it, use it, and reap the benefits for the rest of your life. It is definitely well worth the effort.

This BS best suits a six-deck shoe, where doubling any two cards (even after splitting) and surrender are both permitted, i.e., the most common game offered today. This single chart was carefully compiled from a myriad of others because it alone allows for all the rules that exist in most casinos nowadays. Fortunately, it also represents less than 0.05% advantage loss if used under any other playing conditions. Learning BS thoroughly, therefore, is your first task, before you can hope to become a consistent winner at blackjack. This point cannot be stressed too much. Committing BS to memory will come more easily if you know why the specific plays are recommended, rather than simply trying to remember them by rote. As with the "New Math," understanding is the key to most useful knowledge, and this especially applies to correct BS. Therefore, let us now examine the BS proclamations line by line. Even experienced players should find this exercise helpful, if only as a quick review.

# The Basic Strategy (BS) Chart

## The DEALER is showing a:

| YOU have: | 2 | 3 | 4 | 5 | 6 | 7 | 8 | 9 | T | A |
|---|---|---|---|---|---|---|---|---|---|---|
| 5–8 | H | H | H | H | H | H | H | H | H | H |
| 9 | H | D | D | D | D | H | H | H | H | H |
| 10 | D | D | D | D | D | D | D | D | H | H |
| 11 | D | D | D | D | D | D | D | D | D | H |
| 12 | H | H | S | S | S | H | H | H | H | H |
| 13 or 14 | S | S | S | S | S | H | H | H | H | H |
| 15 | S | S | S | S | S | H | H | H | G | H |
| 16 (not 8s) | S | S | S | S | S | H | H | G | G | G |
| 17–21 | S | S | S | S | S | S | S | S | S | S |
| 17 (soft)* | H | H | H | H | H | H | H | H | H | H |
| 18 (soft)* | S | S | S | S | S | S | S | H | H | H |
| A, 2 or A, 3 | H | H | H | D | D | H | H | H | H | H |
| A, 4 or A, 5 | H | H | D | D | D | H | H | H | H | H |
| A, 6 | H | D | D | D | D | H | H | H | H | H |
| A, 7 | S | D | D | D | D | S | S | H | H | H |
| A, 8 or A, 9 | S | S | S | S | S | S | S | S | S | S |
| 2, 2 or 3, 3 | P | P | P | P | P | P | H | H | H | H |
| 4, 4 | H | H | H | P | P | H | H | H | H | H |
| 6, 6 | P | P | P | P | P | H | H | H | H | H |
| 7, 7 | P | P | P | P | P | P | H | H | H | H |
| 8, 8 | P | P | P | P | P | P | P | P | P | P |
| 9, 9 | P | P | P | P | P | S | P | P | S | S |
| A, A | P | P | P | P | P | P | P | P | P | P |

H = Hit   S = Stand   P = sPlit   D = Double-Down
G = Give up (i.e., surrender if allowed, otherwise hit)

  1. Never take insurance.
  2. Never split 5s or T's.
  * Always hit soft hands totalling 17 or less, whenever doubling-down is not an option. Notice that A,7 is a soft 18, but one with doubling potential. Stand with soft 19s and 20s against any dealer up-card.

## BS Rationale Line by Line

**The DEALER is showing a:**

| YOU have: | 2 | 3 | 4 | 5 | 6 | 7 | 8 | 9 | T | A |
|-----------|---|---|---|---|---|---|---|---|---|---|
| 5–8       | H | H | H | H | H | H | H | H | H | H |

This line is probably obvious to everyone, but let's make sure of our format. For visual clarity, the dealer's stiff up-cards (2 to 6) have been slightly separated from his pat up-cards (7 to A). As before, "T" stands for any ten-valued card, whether it is a true 10 or one of the face cards. Your total is always to be considered "hard" (i.e., when you hold no Aces, or when you must count your Aces as 1s to avoid going over 21), and not made up of a pair, unless noted as such.

The smallest two-card total you could possibly have is 5 (aside from a pair of 2s, which is seen lower in the chart), so you should hit, no matter which card the dealer is showing, since taking another card cannot possibly hurt you. With a total of 5, 6, 7 or 8 you can usually improve your position by taking another card. There is no way you can bust, and by standing with these poor totals the only way you can win is if the dealer busts. Notice that none of these totals is strong enough to warrant doubling your bet against any of the dealer's up-cards.

**The DEALER is showing a:**

| YOU have: | 2 | 3 | 4 | 5 | 6 | 7 | 8 | 9 | T | A |
|-----------|---|---|---|---|---|---|---|---|---|---|
| 9         | H | D | D | D | D | H | H | H | H | H |

Imaginary bells and whistles should ring in your ears whenever you receive an initial total of 9, 10 or 11. The hard two-card total of 9 represents your first good chance to make some "easy" money, simply by doubling your bet.

Don't double your 9 against pat up-cards. When the dealer is showing stiff cards, double-down; otherwise, just take a hit. Note the exception is 9 versus 2. A dealer will always tend to draw stronger totals when showing the lowly 2. More about this later.

The reasoning behind the doubling proposition here is that both you and the dealer will likely draw a T, since approximately one-third of each deck consists of 10-valued cards. "The 10-factor," a handy term coined by Avery Cardoza, suggests that you should always assume the next card to appear will be a T. Therefore, considering this 10-factor, you will most likely end up with a total of 19 after your next card, which represents a fairly strong hand. The dealer will have to draw a third card to his stiff totals of 13, 14, 15, and 16, and hence very likely bust. You will then be paid twice your initial wager as a result of your doubling-down. Taking full advantage of such "proposition" bets is an essential part of BS play. In order to help eliminate the casinos' built-in odds advantages, you *must* increase the size of your bet whenever your chances of winning are better than the dealer's.

**The DEALER is showing a:**

| YOU have: | 2 | 3 | 4 | 5 | 6 | 7 | 8 | 9 | T | A |
|---|---|---|---|---|---|---|---|---|---|---|
| 10 | D | D | D | D | D | D | D | D | H | H |

This situation shouldn't require much thought or explanation. Obviously, with a starting total of 10, doubling-down tends to gravitate toward final totals of 20, which are very strong hands indeed.

However, when the dealer has a 10-valued card or an Ace exposed, it is not wise to double your bet. Showing a T, he will likely end up with a 20 as well. You'd be foolish to shove out more money when the best you could hope for would be a push. You have no advantage in this situation, so risking more money is not justified. With an Ace as an up-card, the dealer usually makes a very strong total, especially if you are playing where soft 17s must be hit. The risk of your drawing a non-T and losing twice your initial wager simply does not warrant doubling-down against these two most powerful dealer up-cards. So, when you have 10 and the dealer is showing anything other than a T or Ace, be sure to double your bet. If you don't, you are passing up a good opportunity to make some extra cash.

**The DEALER is showing a:**

| YOU have: | 2 | 3 | 4 | 5 | 6 | 7 | 8 | 9 | T | A |
|---|---|---|---|---|---|---|---|---|---|---|
| 11 | D | D | D | D | D | D | D | D | D | H |

You have just received a two-card total of 11. Hear the music? See the flashing lights? Hopefully, they are not merely emanating from a nearby slot machine! The imaginary bells and whistles are tolling potential double profits on this hand. Double-down against everything except the dealer's Ace. Next to a blackjack, this is the best starting hand you can get. If you happen to find a single-deck game, double your 11 versus the Ace as well. (See chapter 7 for details on this type of modification to BS.)

When the dealer gets an Ace, he will win about 66% of the time and bust only 12%, because of the Ace's "double-count" potential. Although the dealer does not win two out of three times when you have 11 versus A, according to computer simulations it is still not worth taking the chance of doubling your bet in this case, and possibly losing twice your initial wager.

It is important to note here that in charity casinos or in Europe, where the dealer's hole card is not checked immediately, you would have the additional chance of losing if the dealer flips over a blackjack! Doubling 11 versus A in one of these casinos is even more risky and inadvisable.

### The DEALER is showing a:

| YOU have: | 2 | 3 | 4 | 5 | 6 | 7 | 8 | 9 | T | A |
|-----------|---|---|---|---|---|---|---|---|---|---|
| 12        | H | H | S | S | S | H | H | H | H | H |

You must realize that all your stiff totals from 12 to 16 are losing hands. Face the fact that no matter what you do, when dealt a surplus of stiff beginning totals you will not win much over the long haul. Don't kid yourself; expect to lose in these situations, and at least you'll never be disappointed. In order to minimize your losses, the best you can do is always play BS odds correctly and merely hope for the best.

Normally, your stiff hands warrant standing versus all of the dealer's stiff up-cards, even though on average the dealer will end up with pat hands 72% of the time after initially showing potential stiffs. The fact that he busts 40% of the time means that you win 40% of your hands by standing, rather than risking possible automatic defeat by hitting and consequently busting.

The underlying math gets a little complicated here; even though you have almost a 60% chance of bettering your stiff totals by hitting, you will not necessarily win most of these "improved" hands. Drawing an Ace, 2, 3, or 4 to your 12 doesn't help one iota, since you'll still be stuck with a stiff hand after such hits. While it is true that by standing you only win when the dealer goes over 21, you will win more often by standing than by hitting in these double-stiff situations. When both you and the dealer are showing stiffs or potential stiffs, think to yourself, "If

I hit this hand, I will probably bust due to the 10-factor and lose automatically. But if I stand, the dealer will likely bust after being forced to draw a third card; therefore, I am more apt to win in this situation merely by standing!"

Notice that the only exception to this general rule occurs when the dealer is showing a 2 or 3 and you have a 12. Because less than one-third of all possible draws can actually hurt you (i.e., only the T's), and the dealer will draw a pat hand more than two-thirds of the time when showing a 2 or 3, you should therefore chance a hit in these two cases, even though only a 5, 6, 7, 8, or 9 will actually improve your total. From a neutral shoe, you can easily see, there are four more cards per deck that could indeed help you, as opposed to those seemingly omnipresent T's, which would create an immediate loss.

### The DEALER is showing a:

| YOU have: | 2 | 3 | 4 | 5 | 6 | 7 | 8 | 9 | T | A |
|-----------|---|---|---|---|---|---|---|---|---|---|
| 13 or 14  | S | S | S | S | S | H | H | H | H | H |

Notice that your total of stiff 13 or more does not warrant the risk of a hit against any of the dealer's stiff cards—even a 2 or a 3.

However, since the dealer breaks only about 25% of the time when showing a pat up-card, hitting your stiff totals under these circumstances is always the mathematically correct thing to do. Understand that you will still lose most of these hands, but you will reduce your losses by hitting rather than by standing in the long run. You are about to lose anyway, so you may as well take the opportunity of possibly drawing a small card, which will provide you with a pat and therefore potentially winning hand. This will happen rarely, but more often than the dealer will bust; therefore, you must take the chance of a hit.

### The DEALER is showing a:

| YOU have: | 2 | 3 | 4 | 5 | 6 | 7 | 8 | 9 | T | A |
|-----------|---|---|---|---|---|---|---|---|---|---|
| 15        | S | S | S | S | S | H | H | H | G | H |

If you are allowed to surrender, give up your 15 against the dealer's T to get half of your initial wager back. It has been proven conclusively that hitting 15 versus 10 results in more losses than wins for the player, all other factors being equal. Therefore, giving up half of your bet is your best option. If you are playing where surrender is not offered, then hit versus the dealer's 10, knowing very well that you will likely lose, but also realizing that you are even more likely to lose by standing with the extremely weak 15.

### The DEALER is showing a:

| YOU have: | 2 | 3 | 4 | 5 | 6 | 7 | 8 | 9 | T | A |
|-----------|---|---|---|---|---|---|---|---|---|---|
| 16 | S | S | S | S | S | | H | H | G | G | G |

Similarly, if you can surrender your 16 versus 9, 10, or A, you should do so. Otherwise, take the hit versus these up-cards. Remember that hard 16 is absolutely the worst beginning total that you can possibly get, so don't ever expect to win with it—although you will occasionally by taking the additional card, in spite of the overwhelming odds against you. In this case, as with all your other stiff hands versus pat dealer up-cards, you are merely making the most intelligent play in a losing situation, and thereby reducing your long-term losses.

### The DEALER is showing a:

| YOU have: | 2 | 3 | 4 | 5 | 6 | 7 | 8 | 9 | T | A |
|-----------|---|---|---|---|---|---|---|---|---|---|
| 17–21 | S | S | S | S | S | S | S | S | S | S |

Never hit a hard pat hand versus any dealer up-card. The odds of improving these totals are far too slight, considering your high probability of busting.

For example, even though you will never win with a lowly 17 (unless the dealer actually breaks), the chance of your going over after a hit is greater than the dealer's breaking potential. Besides, you often end up with a push by standing, and sometimes even a surprising win instead of the outright loss that would probably result from hitting any of these pat beginnings.

### The DEALER is showing a:

| YOU have: | 2 | 3 | 4 | 5 | 6 | 7 | 8 | 9 | T | A |
|-----------|---|---|---|---|---|---|---|---|---|---|
| 17 (soft) | H | H | H | H | H | H | H | H | H | H |
| 18 (soft) | S | S | S | S | S | S | S | H | H | H |

A soft 17 (comprised of three or more cards, not A,6) is too weak *not* to hit versus any up-card shown by the dealer. You have no chance of busting by taking the hit in this instance, and you can only win with soft 17 if the dealer goes bust. Realize that any 17 is a very poor total. A hard 17 is bad enough, but when it is soft you rarely hurt yourself by taking another card. Your chances of improving the hand are always much greater, since you will have a second chance to hit again if you happen to pull a stiff total on your first try. Never think of soft 17 as a pat hand. Just as it is advantageous for the casino when a dealer must hit soft 17s, so it is for the player to never stand with this poor total.

Drawing a soft hand of 17 or 18 (when doubling-down is no longer an option) is a common occurrence. Players often handle this situation incorrectly, since the dealer may call out the totals as simply "17" or "18," instead of "7 or 17" and "8 or 18" as is the proper protocol. You might just hear the apparently pat total of 17 or 18 and wave off a hit automatically, without appreciating that such soft hands are very different from their hard counterparts. You are selling yourself short unless you learn to play these hands in the best possible manner.

The soft 18 (as opposed to A,7 when doubling is still an option) is probably the most commonly misplayed hand in all of blackjack. Otherwise competent players will often hit these hands versus the dealer's stiff cards, thinking that the hit can't hurt them, or they will stand with such 18s versus 9, 10, or A. These are both poor plays.

At first glance it might seem reasonable to hit a soft 18 versus the dealer's 3, 4, 5, or 6. After all, BS requires doubling against these stiff up-cards. What most players fail to realize is that doubling in these circumstances actually results in slightly more losses than wins. (See chapter 4 for details.) It is only advisable to double soft 18s when possible because the player wins twice the original wager on winning hands and is therefore further ahead overall. But taking another card without utilizing the doubling proposition is ultimately placing yourself in a losing situation over time in these cases. Don't do it.

Because of the 10-factor and the Ace's double-count potential for the dealer, a soft 18 must be considered a losing hand against the dealer's 9, 10, or A. You should try to improve your prospects in these instances by hitting until you get a pat hand, even though you run the risk of possibly going bust after the second draw. It's definitely worth the gamble versus these strong dealer up-cards.

**The DEALER is showing a:**

| YOU have: | 2 | 3 | 4 | 5 | 6 | 7 | 8 | 9 | T | A |
|---|---|---|---|---|---|---|---|---|---|---|
| A, 2 or A, 3 | H | H | H | D | D | H | H | H | H | H |

Although the general rule is to hit all soft totals, here are a few exceptions that can certainly make you extra cash. Whenever you receive a two-card soft 13 or 14 against the 5 or 6, take advantage of these two weakest dealer's up-cards by doubling your bet. You will have no chance of busting, while the dealer likely will. Very often you will end up with a hard 13 or 14 because of the 10-factor, but sometimes you will draw a 3, 4, 5, 6, 7, or 8 and wind up with a pat hand.

**The DEALER is showing a:**

| YOU have: | 2 | 3 | 4 | 5 | 6 | 7 | 8 | 9 | T | A |
|---|---|---|---|---|---|---|---|---|---|---|
| A, 4 or A, 5 | H | H | D | D | D | H | H | H | H | H |

Soft 15s and 16s gravitate toward stronger totals when hit than do soft 13s and 14s, since the higher the beginning total you receive, the higher your final result will be, generally speaking. Double these soft hands against the dealer's 4, as well as the 5 and 6.

**The DEALER is showing a:**

| YOU have: | 2 | 3 | 4 | 5 | 6 | 7 | 8 | 9 | T | A |
|---|---|---|---|---|---|---|---|---|---|---|
| A, 6 | H | D | D | D | D | H | H | H | H | H |

Players who merely stand on soft 17s are giving their money to the casinos needlessly. Remember, you cannot win with any 17, unless the dealer busts. A,6 is not your usual 17. Whenever the option is available, double against all dealer stiff cards except the 2. As with your beginning two-card total of 9, the 2 often provides the dealer with too strong a final total to risk doubling against it. The 2 is sometimes referred to as "the dealer's Ace" in these situations, since it is such a good starting total for the house.

**The DEALER is showing a:**

| YOU have: | 2 | 3 | 4 | 5 | 6 | 7 | 8 | 9 | T | A |
|---|---|---|---|---|---|---|---|---|---|---|
| A, 7 | S | D | D | D | D | S | S | H | H | H |

A,7 is the most difficult commonly received hand to play correctly. Rest assured that wrong advice will be offered freely to you by well-intentioned players and dealers alike, whenever you are dealt these cards.

Standing against the 2 is wise, since the 2 very often generates powerful totals for the dealer, and drawing to 18 could result in a stiff hand for you, i.e., an even worse situation. The 2 is simply too dangerous an up-card to risk offending in this case.

With dealer up-cards of 3, 4, 5, and 6, however, doubling is justified, since the dealer will bust with these beginning stiffs more often than you will end up with stiffs from your double-downs. Strange as it seems, even though you will lose more hands than you win, you will end up ahead financially by doubling. (See chapter 4 for more details.)

The soft 18 already beats the dealer's potential 17 and ties his 18, so stand versus the 7 and 8.

As mentioned above, because of the 10-factor and the Ace's two-count potential, you know that 18 is a losing hand against the dealer's 9, 10, and Ace. You must try to improve your prospects in this situation by hitting until you get a pat hand or until you break. Keep in mind that many other hands can produce a soft 18 total: A,2,5; A,3,A,3; 4,A,A,2; etc. Standing with such soft hands versus the dealer's strong 9, 10, or Ace is the most common BS crime regularly committed by otherwise law abiding players.

### The DEALER is showing a:

| YOU have: | 2 | 3 | 4 | 5 | 6 | 7 | 8 | 9 | T | A |
|-----------|---|---|---|---|---|---|---|---|---|---|
| 2, 2 or 3, 3 | P | P | P | P | P | P | H | H | H | H |

Splitting is another example of proposition betting that has to be utilized to full advantage if you hope to offset the casinos' inherently favorable odds in the game of blackjack. Since the probability is higher that the dealer will bust when showing stiff cards, splitting your poor beginning totals of 4 and 6 into two separate hands, with the possibility of receiving a favorable second card on each that could provide doubling-down opportunities, is a wise move. It more than doubles your odds of big wins in these situations.

Splitting 2s and 3s even against the dealer's 2 is a smart decision, because of the good chance that you will draw second cards that will produce new beginning totals of 9, 10, or 11 and thereby allow you to double-down. Splitting these pairs against the dealer's 7 may initially look like a questionable play, but the 7 usually results in the dealer's weakest standing total. Believe it or not, a 17 is even weaker in the long run than stiff cards of 5 or 6 for the dealer. Therefore, even though the dealer will often make the pat total of 17, you will make stronger totals by splitting 2s and 3s, and enjoying the possible doubling and additional splitting opportunities, than you would by merely hitting these weak initial hands. As noted earlier, just as they do for the dealer, 2s and (to a lesser extent) 3s tend to produce strong totals for the player as well.

| | The DEALER is showing a: | | | | | | | | | |
|---|---|---|---|---|---|---|---|---|---|---|
| **YOU** have: | **2** | **3** | **4** | **5** | **6** | **7** | **8** | **9** | **T** | **A** |
| 4, 4 | H | H | H | P | P | H | H | H | H | H |

The doubling potential of two hands of 4 each is just barely great enough to justify splitting your fairly weak total of 8 against these two weakest of dealer up-cards.

Note here that you never split 5s, since 10 is nearly your strongest starting total. Because of the 10-factor, your chances of busting with a 5, even against the dealer's weakest stiff cards, are far too great to warrant breaking up a winning initial draw of 10. You must favor the 10's doubling potential. You are always far more likely to increase your winnings by doubling-down on a 10 than by splitting a pair of 5s.

| | The DEALER is showing a: | | | | | | | | | |
|---|---|---|---|---|---|---|---|---|---|---|
| **YOU** have: | **2** | **3** | **4** | **5** | **6** | **7** | **8** | **9** | **T** | **A** |
| 6, 6 | P | P | P | P | P | H | H | H | H | H |

Unfortunately, there is no way to make a silk purse out of a sow's ear. Accept the fact that 6,6 is generally a losing hand any way you play it. Splitting your 6s against all of the dealer's stiff up-cards, however, is a slight improvement over playing your 12 according to normal BS. Even with the split, your only real hope lies in drawing a 3, 4, or 5 to your 6s, then doubling-down. Splitting 6s often results in one lost hand and one winner—a break-even situation that should be appreciated. When you don't lose with 6s, consider yourself a winner.

**The DEALER is showing a:**

| YOU have: | 2 | 3 | 4 | 5 | 6 | 7 | 8 | 9 | T | A |
|-----------|---|---|---|---|---|---|---|---|---|---|
| 7, 7      | P | P | P | P | P | P | H | H | H | H |

This is a poor hand as well. Splitting 7s tends to give you two hands of 17—winners only if the dealer busts. But the greater busting potential of the dealer when showing stiff totals makes splitting your 14 up to 7 somewhat more profitable. At least your 17s will push the dealer's potential 17s. Splitting 7s up to and including 7 is your best option under these circumstances.

You will lose less in the long run by hitting 7,7 against the 8 through A, rather than splitting versus these stronger dealer up-cards. By just standing, you will more than likely lose, so you must try to improve your total in this situation, just as you would with any odd-card beginning total of 14.

**The DEALER is showing a:**

| YOU have: | 2 | 3 | 4 | 5 | 6 | 7 | 8 | 9 | T | A |
|-----------|---|---|---|---|---|---|---|---|---|---|
| 8, 8      | P | P | P | P | P | P | P | P | P | P |

A beginning total of 16 is a player's worst nightmare. The advantage of splitting your 8s against all the dealer's up-cards to 7 is fairly obvious. Two potential winning hands of 18 each (because of the 10-factor again) is far better than sticking with a losing 16 or than risking a bust by taking a hit. In splitting 8s versus the dealer's 8, you are hoping desperately for a push; this is the one and only time you should ever risk more money in the off-chance of merely obtaining a tie.

The wisdom of splitting 8s against the 9, 10, and Ace is not as clear. At first glance, apparently you would be turning one potentially losing hand of 16 into two hands of 18! In reality, however, there is a slight gain in splitting, rather than hitting the easily bustable 16. Quite often you will win one hand and lose the other, resulting in an overall no-loss situation. This is somewhat of an improvement even over surrendering. When you do come out of such a scenario with a tie, consider yourself fortunate.

There is an exception to the "Always split 8s" rule. When playing at charity casinos or outside North America, where the dealers do not take hole cards, surrender your 8s versus the dealer's T and Ace, if allowed. If surrendering is not permitted, then hit your 16 instead of splitting it against these two strong dealer up-cards. In these rare cases, you don't want to take the chance of the dealer turning over a blackjack and your losing two bets instead of one.

| | **The DEALER is showing a:** | | | | | | | | | |
|---|---|---|---|---|---|---|---|---|---|---|
| **YOU have:** | 2 | 3 | 4 | 5 | 6 | 7 | 8 | 9 | T | A |
| 9, 9 | P | P | P | P | P | S | P | P | S | S |

Splitting 9s against all dealer up-cards except the 7, 10, and Ace makes perfect sense. Although 18, in itself, will generally win over the dealer's stiff up-cards and 7, by splitting 9,9 into two hands you seize the opportunity to get more money onto the table precisely when you have a bigger advantage. Both of your hands will gravitate toward the strong total of 19, representing potential winners over everything up to the dealer's own 9, which itself would likely produce a push. There is also the off-chance of drawing a 2 as the second card on each 9, thereby setting up ideal doubling situations.

Do not, however, risk a "sure" win with your initial 18 when the dealer's up-card is a 7. You must assume the dealer will draw a T, so doing nothing in this case should make you a winner.

Obviously, splitting the 9s would not tend to produce winning hands against the T or Ace, so stick with your original 18 versus those two up-cards. The best you can do is hope the 10-factor won't come into play with the dealer's T, but that it will with the Ace in order to force a third-card dealer bust.

| | **The DEALER is showing a:** | | | | | | | | | |
|---|---|---|---|---|---|---|---|---|---|---|
| **YOU have:** | 2 | 3 | 4 | 5 | 6 | 7 | 8 | 9 | T | A |
| A, A | P | P | P | P | P | P | P | P | P | P |

"Always split Aces," as the saying goes, because 11 is your best starting total. Remember that you normally get just one card on each, and resultant "blackjacks" count only as 21s, so don't look for the 3-to-2 payoff when you win. (A blackjack occurs only when your original hand consists of a 10-valued card and an Ace. "Blackjacks" on split Aces are not true blackjacks, since your first two cards of the hand were actually Aces.) Even so, you are much further ahead splitting them than by merely hitting your 2 or 12.

There is, however, one exception to the rule. As with the 8s, when playing at charity casinos or in Europe, where the dealers do not take hole cards, just hit your Aces, rather than splitting them when the dealer also shows an Ace. Keep in mind that a 2 is not such a terrible beginning total. In these cases, it is more than likely that the dealers would draw T's, thereby producing blackjacks. You would end up losing both your split bets, whether or not you drew T's to them. Fortunately, in most North American casinos where hole cards are not checked, the player who splits or doubles-down against the dealer's Ace or T only loses his one original wager whenever the dealer ends up with a blackjack.

Remember never to take insurance unless you are tracking (counting) the cards. It is a poor bet unless the true count (TC) is quite favorable. (For specific information about when you should take insurance, see chapters 4 and 7.)

Also, never split 5s under any circumstances—even if you are a card-counter. You are always better off simply doubling the 10, since the 10-factor tends to produce two totals of 15 from two 5s, in effect turning one winning hand into two losing hands.

Do not split T's unless you are counting the cards and know that the odds of drawing T's are greatly in your favor. (See the MBS-4 chart in chapter 7 for the specifics.) Stick with your already strong total of 20, and be content with the single win.

It is very important that you learn all of the proper BS plays and always play completely accurately. Remember that playing even 5% of your hands incorrectly swings the overall percentage advantage well back into the casino's favor. Never rely upon hunches or intuition. Stick doggedly to the best, mathematically proven strategy available today, and at least give yourself the opportunity to be an overall winner by abiding with correct BS. Simply by following BS consistently, you can rightly think of yourself as a good blackjack player. Even if you learn no additional skills, this is a significant accomplishment, since you will no longer need to fear losing money from the game.

I can't emphasize strongly enough the vital importance of seriously studying the BS table I have provided. If you ever wish to have a significant edge over any blackjack game, or if you plan to read on and eventually learn how to obtain up to 10% advantage over most casinos by using the information and skills presented in subsequent chapters, you simply *must* commit this basic playing strategy information to memory first. If I have dwelled too long upon how very important mastering BS is, please forgive me. But how else can I stress the absolute necessity of learning optimum BS? Please, don't put it off. Perhaps you might like to start with a review right now!

An excellent way to learn the BS of blackjack is by absorbing the reasoning behind each play, as presented in the line-by-line commentary above. Do this even before proceeding to subsequent chapters. The rest of this book can do you little good if you don't know the proper way to play every possible hand that you may be dealt. Study the BS table, section by section, until you feel completely sure of each correct play. Get someone to quiz you by asking questions like, "You have an Ace and a 3, and the dealer is showing a 4. What should you do?" It's not going to be easy, but it is absolutely essential that you completely master all of the best basic plays before trying to incorporate any of the additional information that follows.

From my years of observation, it is a conservative guess that fewer than 5% of all blackjack players play correctly, i.e., have taken the time and made the effort to learn proper BS. Most have a general grasp of what to do, but they end up relying upon their "gut feelings" for the rest. For example, by their frequency of occurrence, over 80% of all playing decisions are covered under the following half-dozen general BS rules:

1. Hit all your stiffs versus the dealer's pat up-cards.
2. Always stand upon receiving a pat total.
3. Stand on all your stiffs versus the dealer's stiff up-cards.
4. Hit all soft totals less than 19.
5. Always split Aces and 8s, but never 5s nor T's.
6. Double-down on all two-card totals of 10 or 11.

As you will see if you check back to the BS chart, only one of the above general BS rules is 100% valid. (As a little review at this point, take a moment now to determine which one it is.) Although they are not entirely accurate, following these six rules puts you far ahead of most players; however, almost 20% of your playing decisions must still be left to chance. This is exactly where the casinos get the advantage that allows them to pay their huge electric bills—and then some! But why should you give away up to 10% of your playing stakes every session by playing these few remaining hands according to only your best intuitive guesses? (I call these players "VIP's," which stands for Viscerally Influenced Players.) Instead, simply learn to play BS 100% correctly regardless of the size of your wager, and enjoy the overall edge for yourself!

## BS Practice Exercises

Work through the following three practice exercises, which increase in difficulty from normal to complex, until you make absolutely no mistakes. None. The answers should come to your mind quickly and effortlessly. The beginning total for each hand is always on the left, and the dealer's up-card is on the right. The BS answer is shown following each example. Do not take this exercise lightly, nor dare to ignore it altogether. You may think you know BS perfectly, so prove it to yourself by covering the answer column with a sheet of paper and jotting down the correct letter codes. Check your results after each group of ten.

The way to make learning most effective is to cover the answers with your finger and expose them only after you finally decide upon each response and actually say it out loud. This sort of immediate reenforcement has been scientifically tested and proven to be the most beneficial in facilitating learning of this type.

Start slowly. Think carefully about the correct BS play for every individual example. Speed is not as important as accuracy at this point, or even later on under actual playing conditions, for that matter. As with almost everything, the more you practice, the easier the job becomes, and therefore the faster you can get at it without losing accuracy. Try to imagine that you are sitting at a blackjack table, having placed your chips in the betting area, and that these are the cards you have just received, in the order they are listed in the exercise.

It has been proven conclusively that people generally play as they practice, so take your practice sessions seriously. You might even choose to make the appropriate "stand" or "hit" hand gestures as you are required to do in a real casino. Try to visualize matching your imaginary bets on required doubles or splits with additional chips. Once you completely master the normal BS practice exercises, proceed to the more complex three-card hands.

The abbreviations used in the exercises are the same as those used in the BS chart earlier in this chapter.

## BS Practice Exercise 1 (Normal)

| Your Hand | Up-card | BS | Your Hand | Up-card | BS |
|-----------|---------|----|-----------|---------|----|
| 7, 5 | 3 | H | 5, 3 | 4 | H |
| 6, 5 | 6 | D | 4, 4 | 7 | H |
| A, 7 | T | H | 5, 4 | 6 | D |
| T, 8 | A | S | 9, 9 | 2 | P |
| 5, T | T | G | A, 2 | 5 | D |
| 8, 7 | A | H | 6, 6 | 6 | P |
| A, 7 | 2 | S | 8, 9 | 5 | S |
| 7, 7 | 7 | P | 9, 7 | 7 | H |
| A, A | A | P | 5, T | 3 | S |
| 4, 6 | 9 | D | A, 6 | 2 | H |
|   |   |   |   |   |   |
| T, 6 | 9 | G | 2, 6 | 5 | H |
| 7, 4 | 2 | D | A, 6 | 7 | H |
| 3, 3 | 8 | H | 4, 4 | 6 | P |
| T, 9 | A | S | 2, 8 | 8 | D |
| A, 6 | 3 | D | 2, 7 | 2 | H |
| 8, 8 | 9 | P | A, 8 | 6 | S |
| A, 7 | 7 | S | 7, 9 | T | G |
| 3, A | 6 | D | 7, 7 | 4 | P |
| 8, 8 | 9 | P | 9, 9 | 7 | S |
| 7, A | 3 | D | 7, 3 | T | H |
|   |   |   |   |   |   |
| 6, 6 | 2 | P | 9, A | 5 | S |
| 2, 7 | 3 | D | T, 4 | 8 | H |
| 3, T | 5 | S | 4, A | 4 | D |
| 2, 2 | 7 | P | 4, 6 | A | H |
| 7, A | 8 | S | 4, 4 | 5 | P |
| 3, 3 | 6 | P | 5, 4 | 5 | D |
| 9, 2 | T | D | A, 6 | 8 | H |
| 9, 9 | 8 | P | 8, 8 | T | P |
| 6, A | T | H | 9, 7 | A | G |
| 7, 4 | 9 | D | 2, 9 | A | H |

# BS Practice Exercise 2 (Difficult)

| Your Hand | Up-card | BS | Your Hand | Up-card | BS |
|-----------|---------|----|-----------|---------|----|
| A, 7 | 9 | H | 7, 7 | 6 | P |
| 9, 9 | T | S | 9, 9 | 9 | P |
| A, A | T | P | 5, 5 | 7 | D |
| 6, T | 2 | S | 5, A | 6 | D |
| A, 6 | 6 | D | 9, 9 | A | S |
| 7, 7 | 8 | H | 6, 6 | 7 | H |
| 4, 4 | 2 | H | 7, A | 6 | D |
| 5, 3 | 6 | H | A, 5 | T | H |
| A, 9 | A | S | 9, 7 | 6 | S |
| A, 7 | A | H | A, 3 | 4 | H |
| | | | | | |
| 5, 5 | 2 | D | 7, A | 5 | D |
| T, 5 | 9 | H | 6, 6 | 5 | P |
| A, 4 | 5 | D | A, 2 | 7 | H |
| T, T | 6 | S | 2, 2 | 5 | P |
| 7, 3 | 6 | D | 8, 3 | 5 | D |
| A, 7 | 4 | D | 9, 3 | 2 | H |
| 3, T | 2 | S | A, 5 | 3 | H |
| 6, A | 4 | D | 7, 8 | T | G |
| A, 4 | 7 | H | 3, 8 | 8 | D |
| A, 6 | 5 | D | 4, 5 | 4 | D |
| | | | | | |
| 7, 4 | 3 | D | T, 5 | 8 | H |
| A, 2 | 2 | H | 6, 6 | 4 | P |
| 4, 6 | 3 | D | A, 3 | 3 | H |
| 7, 7 | T | H | 6, A | A | H |
| 8, A | 9 | S | 9, 7 | 5 | S |
| 5, 5 | 4 | D | 4, 5 | 7 | H |
| 3, 4 | 2 | H | 9, 9 | 6 | P |
| A, 5 | 8 | H | 3, 8 | 8 | D |
| 6, 3 | 4 | D | A, 6 | 9 | H |
| 8, 8 | 8 | P | 6, 9 | T | G |

## BS Practice Exercise 3 (Complex)

| Your Hand | Up-card | BS | Your Hand | Up-card | BS |
|-----------|---------|----|-----------|---------|----|
| 2, 3, A | 6 | H | A, 2, 5 | 8 | S |
| 3, 5, 4 | 2 | H | 9, 5, A | T | H |
| 3, A, 4 | 7 | S | 2, 3, 5 | 9 | H |
| 4, 4, 2 | 4 | H | 4, 2, A | 5 | H |
| T, 2, 5 | T | S | 3, 4, 5 | 3 | H |
| 4, A, 4 | A | S | A, 4, 5 | 3 | S |
| A, 3, 4 | 2 | S | 4, 4, 4 | T | H |
| 5, A, A | 7 | H | 4, 9, 3 | A | H |
| 6, 6, 7 | 9 | S | 2, 2, 9 | 8 | H |
| A, 6, A | 2 | S | A, 4, 3 | 3 | S |
| | | | | | |
| A, 6, A | 9 | H | 5, 3, 3 | A | H |
| 8, 2, A | T | S | 5, A, 5 | 7 | S |
| 2, 4, 5 | 8 | H | 4, A, 3 | 9 | H |
| A, 5, 6 | 4 | S | A, 4, 5 | A | S |
| 2, A, 5 | T | H | 3, 2, 5 | 2 | H |
| 4, 3, 4 | 6 | H | 9, 2, 5 | 6 | S |
| 4, 4, 9 | 3 | S | 6, A, A | T | H |
| 9, 5, A | A | H | 8, 7, A | 9 | H |
| T, 2, A | 3 | S | 3, A, 2 | 5 | H |
| 3, A, 3 | 6 | H | A, 6, A | A | H |
| | | | | | |
| 2, 3, 5 | 6 | H | 7, 6, 3 | 2 | S |
| 5, T, A | 7 | H | 6, 6, 4 | 5 | S |
| 2, 2, A | 8 | H | A, 2, 5 | 3 | S |
| 3, A, 4 | 4 | S | 6, 6, 3 | 9 | H |
| 7, 7, 6 | A | S | 4, 4, 8 | 7 | H |
| 2, 4, 3 | 6 | H | 2, 5, A | 5 | S |
| 3, 4, A | 6 | S | 7, 7, 2 | T | H |
| 6, 6, 4 | 8 | H | A, 3, T | 5 | S |
| A, 2, 3 | 5 | H | 5, 5, 9 | T | S |
| 6, A, A | A | H | 5, A, 5 | 6 | S |

When you can run through the above practice charts fairly quickly without any mistakes, the next step is to move from the abstract to the concrete. (Notice that in exercise 3 you had no option to surrender, split, or double, because after receiving three cards these choices are eliminated.) Since you are now completely comfortable with all BS plays, get a deck of cards and deal yourself at least a thousand random hands while acting as both player and dealer. To prove to yourself that playing according to correct BS actually works, keep a "win/loss" tally sheet to record the results.

Without counting cards, there is no justification for varying the size of your bets. In fact, if you do, the results will be less true due to the fact that you will lose or win more arbitrarily. Just bet one unit, whatever amount you choose it to be, for each hand.

In this exercise, whenever you get a blackjack, credit yourself an extra half-unit on your tally sheet to represent the 3-to-2 payoff that you would receive. Although nothing can help you much when you receive a disproportionate number of stiff hands, the larger the number of trials, the truer the results will be. Be aware that luck, good or bad, can be a big factor in short-term blackjack and easily skews normal results one way or the other, but rest assured that correct BS plays will prevail in the long run. Taking normal fluctuations into account, you should end up with substantial winnings most of the time. The proof of playing proper BS is in the proverbial pudding, so help yourself!

Learning and practicing at home is much easier than in a busy casino. In the beginning, especially, you don't need the usual distractions found there. Nearby slot machines paying off, a crowd of boisterous players whooping it up at a craps table only a few feet away, the glitter from the flashing lights and mirrors in your eyes, the too-loud piped-in music or local entertainment, and the scantily clad cocktail waitresses constantly offering free drinks—these are only a few of the interruptions that you may well have to deal with and must learn to handle in stride. Remember that it can take months, and many practice sessions, to master BS completely. Although there is no substitute for actual experience, more learning can take place in less time in the quiet comfort of your own living room or study area.

Dealing yourself hands, acting as both player and dealer, is an excellent way to practice. If you find that you are weak in some area such as soft hands, make up a gaffed deck that has an extra ten Aces and ten fewer T's in it. "Loading" your practice deck in various ways can emphasize any particular problem upon which you need to concentrate.

Home practice is much easier on the wallet, too. Before putting up real money, you may be wise to hone your skills on one of the excellent blackjack games available for use with your personal computer. If you do, try to get one that at least simulates most of the actual playing conditions that you can expect to encounter in a real casino. The better games allow the player to change the rules, the number of decks used, the number of players at your table, etc. Some even allow you to practice your card-counting skills, by keeping track of the cards as they are brought into play. You need this sort of positive reinforcement regarding the use of BS play, because it will build your confidence and help sustain you through those inevitable losing streaks all of us must endure from time to time.

## BS Questions

Another way to practice BS is to think about the following questions, then check the BS chart to confirm your answers.

When would you double with a beginning total of 9?
When would you split 9s?
When would you double on a T? Against every up-card?
When would you surrender your 16?
When would you double-down with an A,7?
When would you hit your 12?
When would you hit your A,7?
When would you surrender a 15?
When would you double on a two-card 11?
When would you split a pair of 8s?
When would you take insurance if offered?
When would you double-down on an A,6?
When would you stand with A,7?
When would you split 7s?
When would you hit a soft 17?
When would you stand with a three-card soft 18?
When would you split Aces?

When would you double-down with an A,3?
When would you split 6s?
When would you hit an A,5?
When would you hit a three-card soft 18?
When would you double with an A,8 or A,9?
When would you split a pair of 2s?
When would you hit a 14?
When would you double an A,2?
When would you split 4s?
When would you hit an A,4?
When would you double 3s?
When would you stand with A,7?

After a number of winning sessions, perhaps by just playing an appropriate game on your computer, you should be ready to enjoy a few hands with members of your family or friends. When you do, try to adopt a somewhat taciturn demeanor to prepare yourself for actual casino conditions. Exercise restraint, if possible. There is no need to explain everything you know about the game, since your friends or family will probably be more interested in playing for the sheer fun of it. Resist the temptation to "instruct"; unasked-for advice is seldom appreciated and usually detracts from the overall enjoyment of any game. Use poker chips or Monopoly money to keep track of individual winnings. Do not, however, expect to win at every session. Blackjack is often a roller-coaster ride, upon which anything can happen and usually does. Unlike a real roller-coaster ride, though, proper BS and other advice offered throughout this book is enough to insure that you end up at a definitely higher point than where you started.

Only after you can play BS confidently, with 100% accuracy, and when you feel entirely comfortable with all aspects of the game, should you venture into an actual casino. Armed with the complete knowledge of proper BS play, you finally possess the power that all casino personnel genuinely fear, and rightly so: You now have the ability to beat them at their own game.

# 4

# The Myths and Math

Even those readers who are not mathematically inclined should read the first part of this chapter, which dispels the ten most common misconceptions about the game. The last half presents a variety of information and tables likely to be of more interest to those players who enjoy figuring out odds for themselves and understanding the reasoning behind certain plays.

## The Myths of Blackjack

1. Single-deck and multiple-deck games offer the same odds.
2. Expert counting requires a photographic memory.
3. Some bet-ranging systems are better than others.
4. Always play your hands so that you win most often.
5. Never take insurance.
6. Players who play badly can affect other hands.
7. Always split Aces and 8s, but never T's.
8. Surrender is for suckers.
9. Crooked casinos are a thing of the past.
10. Blackjack is a game of chance.

*Myth 1. Single-deck and multi-deck games offer the same odds.*
Many casual players believe that, all other factors being equal, the odds
of winning at a single-deck game are the same as in shoe games. They
figure that, although more decks are used, the same relative number of
cards is still involved; therefore, even for a card-counter, there is no
advantage to playing in one game over the other. In fact, this is not the
case.

Aside from nonmathematical considerations (e.g., single-deck games
are easier to count successfully), Thorp proved that the player's overall
advantage diminishes as the number of decks used in the game
increases. Following proper BS, the player has a 0.13% advantage over
the casino in a single-deck game, but if 5,000 decks were to be used,
then the player would be at a theoretical disadvantage of 0.58% without
tracking the cards. This makes sense because the fewer cards that are
used in a game, the more directly the removal of any finite number of
them affects the distribution or "composition" of the remaining cards.

Consider two imaginary decks, one consisting of only twenty cards,
and the other made up of two thousand cards. Each deck is composed
of half T's and half non-T's. Right after the shuffle, your chances of
drawing a T are an even fifty-fifty, or 50%, from each of these two
hypothetical decks. Now suppose that nine of the T's are removed from
each deck. Your odds of drawing a T as your very next card would be
only slightly over 9% from the small deck (1 out of 11 = 9.1%), but still
almost 50% from the large one (991 out of 1,991 = 49.8%). The more
cards initially involved, the less the remaining pool is influenced by the
removal of specific cards during play. This is one reason your BS play
should change slightly if you move from a multiple-deck to a single-deck
game (see chapter 7 for details). Therefore, since card-counting is a bit
less reliable in shoe games, BS reflects the need to play somewhat
differently in them as opposed to single-deck games.

Another reason to choose a single- or double-deck game as opposed
to a six-deck shoe, whenever the rules are similar, is that you are less
likely to get blackjacks in games that employ more cards. It sounds
incredible, but compare the following two examples mathematically:
(1) In the single-deck game there are 190 (20 × 19 ÷ 2) possible two-
card combinations involving the four Aces and sixteen T's, 64 (4 × 16)

of which produce blackjack; 64 chances out of 190 equals about 34%. (2) In the six-deck shoe, although the ratio of T's to Aces remains 4 to 1, there are 7,140 (120 × 119 ÷ 2) possible two-card combinations involving the twenty-four Aces and ninety-six T's, a total of 2,304 (96 × 24) producing blackjack; 2,304 chances out of 7,140 equals just over 32%.

No wonder most casinos are moving toward offering only six-deck shoe games. Out of every hundred hands composed of Aces and T's that are dealt from a shoe, the expectation of blackjack appearing is nearly two fewer than it is from a hundred similar single-deck hands. Of course, the dealers will also draw the same reduced number of blackjacks in the shoe games, but they can avoid paying the players 3 to 2 on an average of almost one fewer blackjack per shoe, depending upon the number of decks used and how many players are at the table. (The math here allows for considerable discrepancies, but the reader can certainly get the general idea.)

One additional reason that your potential gains decrease in multiple-deck games concerns Modified Basic Strategy (MBS) play, which is detailed in chapter 7. The TC (True Count) tends to stay within narrower limits as the number of decks increases. For example, using only one deck, the TC = 0 only 18% of the time, while for a six-deck shoe the TC = 0 almost 30% of the time. This means that you usually have to wait longer in shoe games for an opportunity to use MBS play at all. Similarly, the TC ranges between −5 and +5 only about 82% of the time in single decks, but it stays within this same limit over 95% of the time in shoe games. This is not good for the counting player, who depends upon the fluctuation of the TC in order to win his larger wagers. The counter's edge increases when he can use MBS plays to full advantage—a job that requires more patience in shoe games.

Although it is slightly more difficult to beat shoe games as opposed to single decks, there are some advantages to playing the shoes. Shoe rules are often better than in hand-held games, dealer cheating is much more difficult to manage from shoes, and because there are so many more multiple-deck games offered, the player has a much greater choice of tables.

The more decks involved, the more the TC tends to stay within narrow limits. A single deck subsequently allows more variance in the

TC than multiple decks. As the TC increases in magnitude, however, this discrepancy is reduced, e.g., the TC will stay between $-10$ and $+10$ virtually 100% of the time, whether you are playing a single- or multiple-deck game. This means that it is unlikely that you will ever encounter a TC beyond $-10$ or $+10$ in any game.

When the TC stays within the $-3$ and $+3$ range (i.e., 86.6% of the time in a six-deck shoe game), your MBS playing gain is only 1.7%, but when the TC ranges from $-6$ to $+6$, for example, your gain climbs to 1.9%. Your MBS advantage varies directly with the magnitude of the TC, whether positive or negative. Therefore, you are more often able to apply MBS with greater success and frequency while playing in single-deck games, as opposed to the more common shoes. It should be evident from this data that double-deck and four-deck games are somewhat preferable to six- and eight-deck shoes with similar rules, for the same reasons.

*Myth 2. Expert counting requires a photographic memory.* When novice players hear the term "counting cards," they conjure up an image of a process that, computer-like, remembers the rank of every card played. From this information mathematical calculations must be quickly made, to determine the best plays to make at any given time. Although miniaturized computers can be used successfully to this end in casinos, they are expensive, difficult to use optimally at the pace of a normal blackjack game, often awkward to conceal, and—last but hardly least—presently deemed illegal. Fortunately, the modern-day counter needs no background in math and only a fair-to-middlin' memory to achieve the desired advantages over any casino blackjack game.

Most professional counters keep just one or two numbers in mind and need to perform only the simplest of mental arithmetic to determine all of their playing decisions. Granted, a few tables need to be carefully memorized, but this can be done well in advance at the counter's convenience. For example, if you can add 6 + 1 and divide by 3 to arrive at the correct rounded-off integer of 2, then you already have the ability to become an expert counter. (See chapter 6 for all the details.)

*Myth 3. Some bet-ranging systems are better than others.* Bet-ranging systems vary from the sublime to the ridiculous. Unfortunately, none is of any real advantage to the player in the long run. Some seem to work better than others in the short term or under specific playing conditions, but not one is of any benefit financially.

Perhaps the most famous betting system ever devised is also the simplest to understand and implement. It has probably occurred to many people independently but is known generally by the name Martingale. Basically, it consists of pocketing all wins, while doubling the size of any lost wagers until a win occurs. The Martingale system is reminiscent of the chronic gambler who always wants to go "double-or-nothing" whenever he or she loses. It is obviously a no-lose situation as long as one can continue to double the size of the bet indefinitely.

The Martingale strategy fails in blackjack because of table limits. For example, whenever you win your initial minimum bet, the winnings are "locked up." But after losing a bet of, say, $10 you must bet $20 on the next hand. If you win, your net winnings total $10, and you start all over by betting the minimum once more. If you lose the second hand in a row, however, you must then bet $40 in an attempt to win $10. An extended losing sequence of wagers would look like this: $10, $20, $40, $80, $160, $320, $640, $1,280, etc. At this point, if the player lost again, a table maximum of $2,000 would not permit the required Martingale bet of $2,560, and therefore the system would fail after eight consecutive losses. This is assuming that no doubled or split hands were called for, which could force the player into limit trouble even sooner. At a $5 to $2,000 table, a series of nine losses in a row would prohibit players from recouping their losses by merely doubling the size of their last bet.

Although such a long string of losses seems highly unlikely to the uninformed, the odds of this happening in blackjack are surprisingly good—especially if the player is not particularly skilled at the game. Even in a fifty-fifty situation such as flipping a coin, the chances of ten heads or ten tails coming up consecutively at any given time are only a little over 500 to 1. Of course, these odds do not indicate when such a series will occur, just its probability. You might flip a coin a hundred thousand times without obtaining ten-in-a-row of anything, or it may happen on your first ten tosses. Similarly, if such a string of ten has just appeared, do not assume that it is unlikely to happen again until another thousand flips have been recorded. Probability theory tells us nothing of the sort.

Once while I was on a break from the blackjack tables I began chatting with an affable old roulette dealer. We started talking about how roulette payout odds are calculated, and how no betting system could ever beat the mathematical advantage of the house in the long run. Our conversation turned to the chance of any one number coming up twice in a row, and the dealer said that he once had the 11 show five straight times. On another occasion he had spun six consecutive greens.

According to the odds, any particular number will appear five times in a row only once out of 2.5 million spins or $(1/38)^4$ on average. For either of the two greens to appear six straight times would require over 3.3 million spins or $(2/38)^5$ of the wheel. I was a little surprised when he mentioned that every few months the whole record-board fills up with all reds or all blacks, with the odd green thrown into the mix. (The roulette record-board, an electronic panel behind the wheel, automatically records the last sixteen numbers that have hit and sometimes displays a number of other statistics as well.) Even allowing the two green numbers to continue the series, it seemed unlikely that this would happen every couple of months or so. I later calculated that theoretically it would require over fifteen thousand spins of the wheel, on average, to achieve such a single string of sixteen-in-a-row losses if one were betting on the opposite color. At an average of three minutes a spin it would take just over thirty-one days to get in fifteen thousand drops of that little white ball. Although it sounded incredible at the time, the dealer was likely telling the truth.

Since no one was playing the wheel and he had an interested listener with whom he could pass some time, the elderly croupier proceeded to relate the following story: Two young men used to come in every Thursday night and play their own version of the Martingale at his wheel. One fellow would always bet black, while the other would stick to the red. If a long series of, say, blacks occurred and the one lad was in danger of running into table-limit trouble, then the other would discontinue his red bets and come to the aid of his buddy by betting the appropriate amount on black to properly continue the Martingale sequence. The two youths were always content to leave each night after making only a few hundred dollars between them.

After about a year of such weekly playing, the roulette dealer figured, the pair must have taken over $10,000 from the casino. Then one

Thursday evening the inevitable finally happened. Reds, with the odd green thrown in, began to fill the record-board. After both men's combined table limit was reached on the even-money outside bets, they began to place chips inside on all of the individual black numbers as well, in order to meet the Martingale's required total wager. A couple more reds appeared and the pair was defeated by the $5,000 table maximum. The dealer claimed to have seen neither of them since.

In his book *Blackjack: A Winner's Handbook* (1990 revised edition), author Jerry Patterson suggests that his readers adopt another bet-ranging regimen to virtually insure that even noncounters walk away from the tables as winners. This magical series of numbers, known as the "Fibonacci Sequence," is generated by adding the two immediately preceding numbers, and therefore looks like this: 1, 2, 3, 5, 8, 13, 21, 34, etc. On page 146, Patterson practically guarantees that you will "score" big winnings by sizing your wagers according to the appropriate Fibonacci number, as follows:

Start with a one-unit bet ($5). If you win the hand and the dealer breaks, move to the next number in the sequence for your next bet. Or, if you win and the dealer does not break, bet the same amount. A double-down or split-pair win would override the dealer nonbreaking hand and allow you to move to the next number in the Fibonacci Sequence, i.e., you win a double-down hand, the dealer does not break, OK to move to the next number in the sequence. If you lose a hand, you move back two levels to get your next bet size, i.e., lose betting 21 units; next hand bet 8 units. If you lose two hands in succession, revert to a one-unit bet. Or, if your bet is above 3 units and you lose a double-down or pair-split hand, you revert to a one-unit bet.

What Patterson fails to realize is that winning and losing streaks occur in every game. When a string of wins happen, the player needs no betting system to come out ahead. By the same token, no bet-ranging system is able to protect the player from a surplus of losses. Just as superstition thrives upon selective memory, betting systems seem to work because we tend to forget the times they fail.

Patterson's book provides reasonable "stop-loss" advice, but just how the novice non-counter is supposed to achieve any big wins in the first place is unclear. Definitely by not staying at "choppy" tables (i.e., where hands are won and lost alternately) according to Patterson, who advises the player to play at only "player-biased" shoes where strings of wins can be expected to occur. If only there were a way to identify such situations in modern casinos, Patterson's "advice" would be worth something.

The late Lawrence Revere felt that another bet-ranging system, the Crayne, was worth mentioning in his book *Playing Blackjack As a Business*, (revised edition, 1996, page 164). This betting system consists of a series of wagers based upon the sequence beginning: 1, 1, 1, 1, 1, 2, 2, 2, 2, 2, 5, 5, 5, 5, 5, 5, etc. Those readers who may be interested in pursuing the study of such bet-ranging systems should do so out of curiosity only, not with any hope of finding an easy way to win. Perhaps too much space here has been devoted to this topic already.

*The Casino Gambler's Guide* by Allan Wilson and *The Theory of Gambling and Statistical Logic* by Richard Epstein are recommended books that, among other things, clearly debunk the myths surrounding betting systems. In short, they prove that no bet-ranging system is superior to one's own intuition. In blackjack, "signs" to sit out a hand or to double the size of your next wager are nothing but old wives' tales which have absolutely no scientific or mathematical justification whatsoever. Only experienced counters can know for certain what cards are more apt to appear next because of probability theory, and therefore they alone can better predict imminent events in the game. Since no one else can possibly foretell how future hands may tend to be skewed from the expected norms, one bet-ranging strategy is just as good (or bad) as any other. None is worth serious consideration. Nevertheless, lucky players will no doubt continue to swear by various bet-ranging systems. Unlucky practitioners will merely swear at them.

*Myth 4. Always play your hands so that you win most often.* This is a not-so-obvious paradox, but BS sometimes requires the player to follow a lower percentage-win strategy in order to maximize overall winnings. For example, suppose as a noncounter you receive an A,7 while the dealer is showing a 6. If you stand with the soft 18 you will win 63% of the time; however, your win percentage will drop to only 59.5% if you double.

Q: What should you do, stand or double-down?

A: Double.

By standing, your win-rate is 26% of your bet (63% − 37%, the dealer's win-rate). By doubling, your win-rate is only 19% (59.5% − 40.5%) of your bet, but you will have twice the money out. You can afford to sacrifice a few points off your win-rate in this case. Twenty-six percent of one single bet is obviously not as good as 19% of a wager twice the size. Although you will lose more often by doubling in this case than by standing, you actually win more money in the long run by adhering to BS.

*Myth 5. Never take insurance.* The only relevant factor when deciding whether or not to take insurance is the probability that the dealer will get a T (a 10-valued card) to go with his Ace. Insurance is truly a proposition bet, which should be considered a completely independent event from whatever your two-card total happens to be. Since the insurance payoff is 2 to 1, it is an even-money situation only when *exactly* one-third ( 33.3%) of the undealt cards are T's. Contrary to the BS edict that one should never take insurance, it is a smart choice for the player when more than a third of the cards remaining to be dealt are T's.

Well-intentioned players and dealers alike will freely advise you to insure a hand of, say, T,T but not one of, say, 2,3. Insuring strong hands while not insuring weak hands makes no sense whatsoever. In fact, just the opposite is true. With a hand of 20, two extra T's must be used up; therefore, the odds are even less likely that the dealer will also have a T in the hole, causing you to be all the more apt to lose your insurance wager.

If you have not been tracking the cards, you have to assume that the ratio of T's to non-T's is that of a freshly shuffled deck (16 to 36, or slightly over 30% T's). Taking into account that the dealer must be showing an Ace to offer the insurance proposition, the ratio of available T's to non-T's climbs to just over 31% (sixteen out of a possible fifty-one), before considering the ranks of your first two cards or those of any other player. It would be necessary to see three more non-T's and no additional T's before the ratio would equal the even-money odds of 33.3% (sixteen out of forty-eight possible draws). But even if you see four more non-T's than T's per deck, the insurance wager is still not a winning one but merely a break-even proposition. Off the top of a fresh deck, there would have to be five or more non-T's than T's remaining to be dealt (bringing the ratio above 33.3%) in order to justify making the insurance wager. Only if you have been counting the cards and know that there are more than four non-T's than T's used up per deck should you consider insurance. Otherwise, join the noncounters and politely decline the offer. (This advice is usually reliable, but see note 4 of the MBS-4 chart in chapter 7 for the exception.)

Many players fail to realize that accepting "even money" for blackjacks is actually the same as taking insurance. Consider the following scenario: Three noncounters are all dealt blackjacks on $10 bets, but the dealer shows an Ace as her up-card. The dealer then asks, "Insurance anyone?" and player 1 slides $5 out into the insurance area of the layout. Player 2 says, "I'll take the even money!" and the dealer immediately gives him $10. Player 3 sits pat as BS dictates. The dealer then flips over her hole card to reveal a non-T and proceeds to resolve the remaining payoffs. Player 1 loses his $5 insurance bet but is paid $15 for his blackjack, which nets him $10 on the hand. Player 2 has already received his $10 even money, netting the same as 1. Only player 3 gets the 3-to-2 payoff ($15 in this case) that a blackjack normally provides. Had the dealer obtained a blackjack as well, player 1 would have received $10 for taking insurance and a push, netting the same amount as player 2, who already pocketed $10 from his even money. Player 3 would push and neither win nor lose.

This example shows that insuring a blackjack and taking the even-money offer always works out to exactly the same result. Beginning players are always tempted to grab the even-money payoff, and often do, without realizing that by doing so they are actually accepting the insurance bet. They never take insurance while holding any other hands, since they are aware that the insurance proposition generally favors the house, but they cannot seem to resist the "sure win" when holding a blackjack. Without knowing the TC, they are unwittingly letting the casinos off the hook, by forfeiting their potential 3-to-2 payoffs, whenever they agree to settle for even money.

***Myth 6. Players who play badly can affect other hands.*** This is a commonly held view among players who have no grasp of probability theory, the law of averages, chance, luck, or odds in general. Many seemingly experienced players believe, for example, that how the third-base player plays his hand influences whether the dealer will draw a pat hand or bust. Or, when someone decides to split T's versus a 6 and then the dealer ends up drawing a 4 or 5 to his 16, resulting in a loss for the whole table, it is not unusual for players to abandon the table in disgust. They figure that the dealer would have gone over 21 if such a "foolish" play had not been made. Seasoned veterans of the game playing one-on-one with the dealer are often indignant when the sequence of "their" shoe is interrupted by someone else joining the game before the shuffle. A large segment of the blackjack-playing public is convinced that a game with weak or beginning players is inevitably doomed to failure.

If this were not such a widely held misconception, it would not deserve serious comment. How otherwise intelligent people can rationalize such a ridiculous concept is difficult to comprehend. Could it be that they actually believe that the dealer has somehow prearranged the cards so that the players will lose? No, because if that were the case it would be necessary for someone to disturb the expected sequence of play in order for the players to win! Possibly these disgruntled players are simply looking for some innocent victim to blame for their own losses, or an excuse to justify their leaving the game. Perhaps they have won sessions in the past in which all of the players were of one mind, and naturally they can vividly recall the rewards of such "good" playing. (Needless to say, they must quickly forget the equal number of wins that result from the "bad" players' draws.) Just as superstition thrives upon such selective memory, so too are formed the unconscious convictions of ignorant blackjack players.

To understand probability theory correctly, we have to imagine a "perfectly" shuffled deck of cards or an "ideal" coin being flipped. Such a coin or deck could never be found in the real world, since there is no such thing as a truly random shuffle outside of a computer, and an actual coin could become worn unevenly on one side or perhaps land on its edge occasionally. Mathematical probability is not concerned with specific events such as a won or lost hand resulting from a particular "good" or "bad" play—although statistics can be compiled in this way and often prove useful. Rather, probability theory refers to the results of an infinite number of similar events or, more precisely, to what happens "in the long run."

Let's assume that the shuffle is a random one and that you will win 50% of your hands by following BS. Let's also assume that you are not counting cards and therefore have no specialized knowledge of what cards are more apt to appear in imminent hands, or the upcoming "dependent sequential events," as mathematicians call them. The "odds" or probability of a win (or loss) remain constant regardless of the number of players at the table or how they play their hands. Similarly, jumping in and out of a game without knowing the count offers no advantage to any player. By doing so you are just as apt to be avoiding beneficial cards as unfavorable ones. (See *The Theory of Gambling and Statistical Logic* by Richard Epstein.) You wouldn't think of crediting a good player for your wins; neither should you consider blaming a poor player for your losses.

It is perhaps appropriate to comment here on another common misconception regarding probability theory. Many players believe that "luck," good or bad, will "even out" eventually. Everyone knows that when flipping a coin the ratio of heads to the number of total tosses will approach a true limit of 50%. This is only common sense. From this knowledge they "reason" that if, say, ten successive heads occur, the next flip will more likely result in tails. Nothing could be farther from the mathematical truth, since every toss has exactly an even chance of being heads *or* tails. Even though the ratio will tend to approximate the theoretical limit more closely as the number of tosses increases, there could very well be an excess of heads indefinitely.

Suppose that after fifty flips of the coin you noticed that twenty more heads appeared than tails, i.e., fifteen tails and thirty-five heads. The ratio of heads to tails would be 70% (35 ÷ 50). The same excess of heads in one hundred tosses would be only 60%, and in a thousand tries (510 heads) only 51%. You can see that, although the true limit is approached as the number of tosses grows, there is no reason to believe that the absolute numbers of heads and tails will tend to equalize themselves. In fact, in his book *An Introduction to Probability Theory and Its Applications,* William Feller proves mathematically the unlikelihood of such a skewed number of coin flips ever evening up.

The same thinking can be applied to blackjack hands played according to BS. Many otherwise intelligent players firmly believe that in a truly fifty-fifty game at an honest table, and all other factors being equal, after losing an excessive number of hands their net losses must diminish due to the "law of averages" if they continue to play long enough under these even-odds conditions. Their logic, however, is tragically flawed. Consider the following hypothetical record sheet:

| Hands Played | Hands Won | Hands Lost | Win Percentage | Net Losses |
|---|---|---|---|---|
| 10 | 3 | 7 | 30% | 4 |
| 100 | 35 | 65 | 35% | 30 |
| 1,000 | 400 | 600 | 40% | 200 |
| 10,000 | 4,500 | 5,500 | 45% | 1,000 |
| 100,000 | 49,000 | 51,000 | 49% | 2,000 |

As seen in this example, according to Feller, although the win percentages will theoretically approach 50% as the number of hands played increases, net losses are actually more apt to increase! This chart supports the laws of probability, specifically the law of large numbers, while illustrating the futility of expecting a trend to reverse itself. There is no good reason to suspect that bad luck will ever turn to good luck or that "it's bound to change eventually!"

*Myth 7. Always split Aces and 8s, but never T's.* According to BS one should always split Aces and 8s, but never T's. Unless you are counting the cards and know the appropriate MBS indices, you should abide by BS rules. But, just because you see players failing to split Aces or 8s, or splitting T's, do not automatically assume that they are making playing errors. They may know very well what they are doing and, more precisely, why they are doing it. For information about when it is wise to go against such BS, see chapter 7.

*Myth 8. Surrender is for suckers.* "Did you come here to gamble, or just to give your money to the house?" grunted the surly old loser next to me, after I surrendered the first three hands I received. I just shook my head in disgust and didn't bother pointing out to him that while I had lost a bet and a half, he had lost his last three wagers entirely. "Surrender is only for suckers, you know," he continued. "Do you think the casinos would offer such a thing if it weren't to their advantage?" Even more beneficial to the player than knowing when to take insurance, surrender is the most misunderstood and least used of the commonly available options. When Atlantic City opened its first casino in May of 1978, its "early" surrendering policy led some knowledgeable players to dub it "the Candy Store." It didn't take the casinos long to realize how beneficial the early surrender was for the players, and in September 1981 they all downgraded "early" to "late" surrender, i.e., offering the surrender option only after the dealer is sure that she has no blackjack. In those intervening years, however, millions of dollars that would otherwise have been lost to the casinos were "surrendered" back to intelligent players.

Taking advantage of correct surrendering opportunities benefits the card-counting player much more than the strictly BS player. While surrendering 15 versus T, and 16 versus 9, T, or A provides the BS practitioner with a slight gain over hitting, knowing the proper MBS surrendering indices and acting upon them can increase a counter's win-rate by up to half a percentage point. (See the MBS-5 chart in chapter 7 for specifics.)

*Myth 9. Crooked casinos are a thing of the past.* There is a general consensus among current blackjack writers that there is far less cheating in today's casinos than there was years ago. Even though this is likely true, it still says nothing about how much cheating still takes place. Once a fully licensed and practicing blackjack dealer myself, now retired, I am well aware of the many ways a dishonest dealer can cheat for the house, for a player, or for himself. Also, knowing what I do about the underworld's past activities, I would be very surprised to learn that its involvement in illegal gambling enterprises has ceased to exist altogether.

Cheating has existed as long as gambling itself. Organized crime exerted a strong influence upon gaming throughout North America long before Bugsy Siegel opened the Flamingo in Las Vegas, December 26, 1946. Some people believe that the "mob's" control and illegal activities have virtually disappeared since the large syndicates took over the mega-casinos during the 1960s and 1970s. However, in a *Rouge et Noir News* interview published in early 1976, an organized crime associate is quoted as follows:

> We have our people in key spots....the elements that were represented by previous owners are still active in Nevada casino

gaming.... Blackjack provides one of our biggest and safest sources of income. We have trained card-counters who are "allowed" to play for large stakes without being barred... the decks don't get shuffled up as often for our players, and house personnel don't overreact to large increases in our bet size. The scam is so simple and effective that we've spawned a bevy of competitors. So many insiders now have working arrangements with card-counters that it has become necessary to bar unaffiliated counters to protect the bottom-line performance.

In this way, or with the help of a skilled "mechanic" (a cheating dealer), large amounts of money can be skimmed off a casino's otherwise legitimate operations even without its owner-syndicate's knowledge. Considering the many reported cases of underworld figures charged with or convicted of various illegal associations with prominent casino management personnel, there can be little doubt of the mob's influence still being very much alive and well in many major casinos.

A dealer need not be a talented magician to cheat the players (or the house) out of hundreds of dollars per shift. The "glamour" of dealing blackjack wears off quickly, and it is understandable that many dealers are drawn into unlawful activities to supplement their meager incomes. Dealers can be coerced into skimming operations or into bilking ordinary players out of their bankrolls in order to increase casino revenues. They sometimes team up surreptitiously with players in order to "help" them leave the tables with their pockets bulging with chips, splitting up the profits later at an appropriate place and time. Wherever the ill-gotten loot goes, it comes from the unsuspecting playing public, since some casinos expect a certain "take" from each table, and dealers whose tables lose are more apt to be let go.

Unfortunately, it is next to impossible to spot a cheating dealer's illegal moves, and even more difficult to prove. If you do suspect that a dealer may be doing more than the automaton's job she was trained to do, there is little point in making a scene. Unless you receive an obviously incorrect payoff for a hand, just move on to an honest table.

This talk of possibly corrupt dealers and casino personnel is certainly not meant to discourage players from pursuing the game of blackjack.

First of all, you should realize that the vast majority of dealers and casino employees are completely trustworthy. (Some casinos have well-known and ruthlessly enforced policies designed to curb any unsavory activities, such as on-the-spot firing of all employees who happen to be working during a shift in which any swindling practices are discovered—not just the guilty parties. This puts a lot more pressure on everyone concerned to make sure there is no thievery of any kind taking place.) After all, casinos don't have to stoop to cheating methods in order to relieve most players of their money. It's a generally known fact that most blackjack players don't have a clue about how to win.

Following are five things you can do to protect yourself from unsafe games:

1. Choose young, inexperienced dealers. Beginning dealers are seldom cheats. The younger the dealer, the less likely he will be a crook. They simply don't have the experience necessary to steal skillfully, nor the inclination to sanguinely pocket a few easy (albeit dishonest) dollars that could put their jobs and training in jeopardy. In fact, surveys have shown that young, good-looking female dealers are the ones most likely to allow you to walk away a winner from blackjack tables. (The reasoning behind this apparent fact is purely speculative, but it purports that pretty, young women dealers are less likely to be "mobbed up" and are usually more interested in attracting compliments and tips than they are in ripping off players.)

2. Play at tables where the players are happy; it's likely to be a sign that they are winning money. This obvious clue that the game is honest is often overlooked. When you see large stacks of chips in front of other players, pull up a seat there yourself.

3. Tip the dealer occasionally. Dealers are not as apt to rip off a regular toker as a skinflint. Sometimes after getting a blackjack, play the "half-bonus" for the dealer. Even as little as a dollar or two bet for the dealer now and then will keep him more favorably disposed toward you. Remember that dealers are not just machines; they have feelings like everyone else. In any case, never be a whiner when you lose, or, even worse, blame the dealer for a poor card or a losing hand. If you commit this unforgivable faux pas, don't be surprised if you "coincidentally" start receiving only bad draws.

4. Play shoe games. It is far more difficult to deal seconds, to stack six shuffled decks, or to perform other common cheating moves on a player (or for a confederate) from a shoe than it is from hand-held single- or double-deck games. ("Seconds" are cards which *should* be dealt *after* the next available card, but are dealt immediately since the dealer knows the very next card and is keeping it for himself or a confederate.)

5. Look for casinos equipped with blackjack-detecting devices. These little electronic eyes eliminate the need for dealers to look under T's or Aces, thereby discouraging possible collusion between a dealer and a player.

Several Las Vegas casinos have been dragging their feet for many years regarding 4 and 5 above. Perhaps the "powers that be" would find it too difficult to steal money from their employers if only shoe games with no-peek devices were used.

*Myth 10. Blackjack is a game of chance.* While there are elements of both luck and skill in blackjack, it can no longer be considered just another game of chance. As in many games, luck and skill are definitely factors. In darts, bowling, and numerous other such activities it is always possible to succeed through sheer luck; however, it is primarily skill that determines the consistent winners. Even so with blackjack; why else would casinos bar any players at all?

By barring counters the casinos are, in effect, welcoming unskilled players to the game with open arms while refusing skillful players the right to play at all. Upon reflection, this is an unconscionable act if they consider blackjack a game of chance, and totally unscrupulous if they believe skill is the determining factor. It's kin to some sleazy carnival barker refusing you (who look as if you might actually be able to throw a ball hard and straight) the opportunity of winning a Kewpie doll. If only losers were allowed to belly up to blackjack tables, even these suckers would eventually learn to avoid the game.

Players at roulette or craps who vary their bet sizes or win money from the games are not denied further access, because management knows that these are games of chance, which mathematically cannot be beaten. If the casinos remain so greedy that they no longer allow a few skilled blackjack players to be winners (whether by restricting the rules or barring counters), then they are threatening the very existence of the game. It has been estimated that less than 2% of their net profits from blackjack are lost to counters. Surely this is an acceptable business write-off as long as it insures the popularity and continuing growth of the industry.

The fact that the game can be beaten through intelligent playing is precisely what draws hordes of gamblers and nongamblers alike to blackjack. Businesspeople who would not normally visit a casino at all are now willing to ply their skills at blackjack, because there is an acceptable risk coupled with the possibility of winning. This is the basic irony of blackjack; the biggest casino moneymaker of all table games is the only one that can be defeated through skillful play.

## The Math and Statistical Facts of Blackjack

As late as the mid-1950s, casino operators knew that they made money from their blackjack tables, but none knew exactly what percentage advantage they enjoyed. In his book, *Card Games, Complete With Official Rules* (1952), Ely Culbertson pointed out: "In no game that has been played for high stakes has there been less analysis of the science of playing than in Black Jack. The only available guide to strategy is empirical; no one has more than his opinion on which to estimate the advantage of the dealer." Thankfully, nowadays adhering to the proper BS plays alone is enough to reward players with a slight advantage in single-deck games.

Correct BS is based entirely upon a player's advantage or disadvantage according to which up-card is showing, i.e., the dealer's busting potential. There are two ways this can be determined: (1) Baldwin et al. spent three years calculating correct BS plays mathematically according to probability theory. (2) Julian Braun developed computer programs that simulated millions of random hands containing every possible combination of cards, then factored in resulting wins, losses, and pushes to establish the best play in each case. The following chart shows this relationship for every possible dealer up-card. Also shown is the dealer's chance of busting with the same up-card. From this data it can be calculated that the dealer will bust 28.36% of the time.

| Dealer's Up-card | Player Win/Loss | Dealer Bust |
|---|---|---|
| 2 | 9.8% | 35.30% |
| 3 | 13.4% | 37.56% |
| 4 | 18.0% | 40.28% |
| 5 | 23.2% | 42.89% |
| 6 | 23.9% | 42.08% |
| 7 | 14.3% | 25.99% |
| 8 | 5.4% | 23.86% |
| 9 | −4.3% | 23.34% |
| T | −16.9% | 21.43% |
| A | −36.0% | 11.65% |

From Thorp's original table, the chart below shows the player's advantage or disadvantage in percent as specific cards are removed from the deck, if the player follows correct BS.

| Deck Composition | Player BS Advantage/ Disadvantage |
|---|---|
| One full deck | 0.1% |
| No 2s | 1.8% |
| No 3s | 2.1% |
| No 4s | 2.6% |
| No 5s | 3.6% |
| No 6s | 2.4% |
| No 7s | 2.0% |
| No 8s | 0.4% |
| No 9s | −0.4% |
| No T's | −8.1%* |
| No Aces | −2.4% |
| 5,000 decks | −0.6% |

*Approximate figure only

We can see that the removal of the Aces from a deck results in a financial loss of 2.4% to the player. But surprisingly, when all four 5s are missing, the player has a gain of 3.6%. Therefore, Aces are not as important as one might think, and 5s are more significant than expected. Note too that 8s and 9s are virtually of negligible benefit to either the house or the player.

## Top Ten Hands

According to Revere's *Playing Blackjack As a Business* (1996), page 86, the house advantage in a single-deck game when no Aces remain to be dealt is 2.59%. On page 70 of the same book, the top ten two-card beginning totals that win the most money are, in order:

1. Blackjack
2. T, T
3. 11
4. T, 9
5. 10
6. A, 9
7. A, 8
8. A, A
9. 9
10. A, 7

Revere does not reveal how his statistics were determined, and some seem questionable, to say the least: for example, 19s usually beating soft 20s?

Neither do Revere's tables on pages 70 and 71 correspond to Braun's charts on pages 82 and 83 of *How To Play Winning Blackjack* (1980), although both claim to indicate a player's chance of getting specific hands, and the odds of winning or losing with such hands. For example, Revere claims T,9 versus T is usually a winner, while Braun shows the same hand loses most of the time. Perhaps mildly interesting for the reader to peruse, none of these tables are reproduced here. (Revere's book was originally published in 1969. Although good for that time and boasting dozens of innovative color-coded tables, the book is not accurate enough for players today even though it has supposedly undergone "revisions" by someone. Revere himself died in 1977. Braun's figures are likely more reliable.)

Hi-Low TC integers for every specific two-card total are given in Stanford Wong's *Professional Blackjack* (1981), pages 166-67.

## Blackjack Versus Other Casino Games

In 1997 alone, Nevada casinos netted an estimated $6 billion, which works out to about $11,415 a minute throughout the entire year. These huge profits are possible because most players are true gamblers. They eagerly bet their money on various casino games that consistently pay off with unfavorable odds. They hope against hope that they will be one of the lucky few who walk away winners. Compare blackjack's favourable playing odds of up to 10% for the player to the advantages that exist for the casino in some of these other popular games:

*Keno (30%).* People play keno, like bingo, for the fun of it, seldom expecting to actually win. They are merely having a "fling" with Lady Luck for the sheer excitement it offers.

*Slot machines (3% to 25%).* According to William Newcott (*National Geographic,* December 1996, page 73), Las Vegas casinos make more money from slots than all of the table games combined. There are over 115,000 machines in Clark county alone. Players beware: Casinos can set their machines to be "loose" or "tight." Some video poker games, however, are purported to be beatable if played correctly long enough.

*Craps (1.4% and up).* This is the ultimate dice game. The low house advantage applies only to the "line bets"; all others take a larger bite out of your bankroll. Certain "odds bets" when combined with the line bets can offer even less than 1.4% casino advantage, and therefore are the best bets available to the player.

*Roulette (1.35% and up).* Most tables have two green numbers, 0 and 00, which increase the casino's advantage to 5.26%, but the European style wheels have only one green zero, which lowers the house odds to 2.7%. Many European games offer *en prison* wagers on the six even-money outside bets. In this case, when the zero hits, a player's bet is merely "imprisoned" until the next spin of the wheel. If the following spin results in a win for the player, he doesn't lose the original wager after all, and the whole bet is returned. The *en prison* rule reduces the house odds to only 1.35%.

*Baccarat (1.17% and up).* Baccarat and mini-baccarat offer the lowest fixed casino percentage-advantage odds for single bets in any game. The player hand has losing odds of 1.37%, while the bank hand offers only 1.17% loss.

## Proposition Bets

Proposition bets are merely proposals whose odds can be determined mathematically. Wagering that Beetle-Balm will show in the third race at Goose Downs is not a proposition bet, but betting that you can flip two heads or two tails in a row is. Unless you know how to figure the odds of such wagers, you are wiser to avoid them. However, as seen earlier in this chapter, being able to calculate the odds of a simple proposition bet like blackjack's insurance is an important asset, and within the ability of most players.

Every roulette or craps bet placed is a proposition bet. The odds of any particular number hitting can be calculated precisely. For example, in roulette the house advantage is determined by the fact that the player wins only once out of thirty-eight tries (i.e., winning thirty-five chips while losing thirty-seven), which means that the casino is up two chips for every thirty-eight spins of the wheel on average ($2/38 = 5.26\%$). Similarly, in craps every payoff is predetermined by the probability ratio of which dice total is most apt to appear. For example, 7 is produced by six possible combinations, but 4 by only three; therefore, the Point 4 odds-bet is paid off 2 to 1.

In blackjack the only true proposition wagers are the insurance and the over/under side bets. A few casinos offer a variation known as the "over and under 13" proposition as follows: According to the total of the player's first two cards, even money is paid if he has bet correctly. For this wager, Aces are counted as 1s only. A total of exactly 13 is a loser, being neither over nor under 13. This is not a smart bet to make unless one is counting the cards and knows the TC is very positive or negative, since there is approximately a 9% chance of two cards totaling exactly 13; therefore, the casino's advantage is a constant 9%. Knowing that the TC is extreme, however, can make this proposition bet a winner.

Think about the coin-flipping example mentioned above. Suppose some stranger offered you 2-to-1 odds if you could obtain two similar results on your first two tosses. If you made two heads or two tails you would win $20, but if you didn't you would lose $10. Would you accept the proposition? Before reading the answer below, try to calculate the odds for yourself.

Since the results of fair coin tosses are exactly even on the average, the chance of getting heads (or tails) for any particular toss is always the same, i.e., 50% or 1-to-1 odds. If your first flip is heads, the odds that you will flip heads on the next toss is still dead even. Similarly, if your first toss is tails, there is a fify-fifty chance that your second toss will also be tails. Therefore, you would be wise to accept such a proposition bet, because the chance of your succeeding only warrants even money, while the stranger was prepared to give you 2-to-1 odds.

The same stranger now suggests to you another proposition bet: he offers even money if you can pull two cards of the same color from a freshly shuffled full deck on your first two tries. Assuming a fair deck in which half the cards are red and half are black, should you accept the wager? As in the coin-flipping example above, it sounds like the chances of succeeding would be exactly even. Right? Wrong. Once you pull out a card, whether it is red or black, there are fewer of that color remaining in the deck than there are of the other color. Your second draw would no longer be a strictly fifty-fifty chance. By accepting such a wager you would be actually giving the stranger odds.

These two examples further illustrate why blackjack can be beaten while other table games cannot. The odds in roulette and craps always remain fixed in favor of the house, and there is nothing the player can do to change them. Blackjack's odds are constantly changing. Sometimes they favor the house, and at other times they favor the player. By observing which cards have already appeared in a blackjack game and playing accordingly, the player can actually improve his chances of winning. Cards, in effect, do have a sort of "memory"; coins, bouncing balls, or rolling dice do not.

Here's a proposition bet you can try on a friend. Suggest the following: "You'll draw two cards from four Jacks and four Aces, and I'll draw two cards from just three Jacks and only two Aces. At $1 a hand, we'll give each other even money for blackjacks, and play until one of us is up $25. Okay?"

Being able to figure out exactly who would have the advantage in this kind of problem is a math skill worth remembering. It goes like this:

From eight cards, consisting of four Jacks and four Aces, there are 28 (8 × 7 ÷ 2) possible two-card combinations. But only twelve of these are not blackjacks—the six made up of only Jacks plus the six made up of only Aces. Therefore, the odds are 16-to-12, or 4-to-3, in favor of drawing a blackjack in this situation, over 57%.

From five cards, consisting of three Jacks and two Aces, there are 10 possible two-card combinations, but only three do not involve the Aces. Of the seven that do, only one combination consists of both Aces, so six combos must be blackjacks. Therefore, 6 out of 10 equals 60% Blackjacks in this case.

Maybe you should reconsider taking "advantage" of your friendship by offering such a proposition.

## A Blackjack Paradox

Now that you have your mathematical thinking cap on, root out the fallacy in logic from the following argument:

At the end of each shoe, when the shuffle card comes out, if the count is very positive it means that a lot of little cards have been used, and therefore the players have been at an overall disadvantage, possibly throughout the entire shoe. But, if the count is very negative at the end of the shoe, it means that more than a normal number of T's and Aces have appeared (which tend to use up fewer cards per hand); therefore, the dealer can squeeze in another round or two before the shuffle— while the players are still at a disadvantage! Therefore, in shoe games casinos must always have the odds in their favor.

No answer is being provided for the above paradox; you are fully capable of solving this one on your own.

Throughout this book I have made a conscious effort to avoid personal anecdotes. Many blackjack publications are absolutely crammed with such items, which, although mildly entertaining, prove absolutely nothing and are basically worthless to the reader. After all, personal testimonies can be paraded out to "substantiate" anything under the sun. While writing the above paragraph, however, I was reminded of a shoe game that I experienced years ago in the casino on

Paradise Island, Bahamas. I believe the incident is worth relating.

While strolling behind various tables one afternoon, I happened to notice one particularly bad shoe. It started out negative and got progressively worse as it neared the end. The TC was −14 when the shuffle card finally came out, and I almost said something to the dealer as he proceeded to deal another round to the almost full table. As I fully expected, he drew a pat hand, and the players lost all of their doubles and splits. None, however, apparently even noticed the shuffle card just lying there beside the discard tray; at least no one commented about this obvious "oversight." When the dealer finally picked it up to start the shuffle, he shot me a sheepish glance. Although I had said nothing out loud, maybe he had picked up on my negative "vibes" somehow, since I was certainly disgusted and amazed at such unabashed audacity. This may have been just an innocent mistake. Alternatively, he may well have been a dealer who could count, and who was instructed to make a little extra money for the house by dealing additional hands whenever the shuffle card came out while the count was very negative.

Earlier in this chapter, the chance of ten heads or ten tails appearing consecutively was said to be just over 500 to 1. The odds of such strings happening are calculated as follows: The probability of two similar consecutive results is dead even, or one out of two attempts. To determine the odds for three-in-a-row, it is necessary to multiply by 2, i.e., one out of four flips. It is seen that for heads or tails to appear $x$ number of times in a row, the probability can be represented by $2^{x-1}$. Therefore, the odds of ten in a row occurring is once every $2^9$ trials, i.e., once every 512 flips. The chance of a roulette record-board filling up with only reds or blacks (and ruining a Martingale, as mentioned earlier in the dealer's story) is considerably less than once every $2^{15}$ spins of the wheel, because of the 5.26% appearance of the greens.

### The Kelly Criterion

Edward Thorp, in his famous *Beat the Dealer*, first applied this mathematical principle to the game of blackjack, although it applies to all wagering situations. Professor J. L. Kelly originally suggested it and proved it mathematically in 1956, and it has been substantiated in practice by computer runs. Basically, the theory is this:

> *The optimal betting method is to bet a percentage of your total bankroll that corresponds exactly to the percent advantage you have at any particular time.*

Known as the "Kelly Criterion," this betting guide seems rather obvious to us today, but it was not always so. Gamblers did not realize that there was a precise relationship between the amount they should bet, their advantage, and their available bankroll. Thanks to the Kelly Criterion, the correct-sized wager can be determined as long as one knows the advantage one enjoys.

## How Rules Affect Player Advantage

According to proper BS, playing in two different casinos does not provide the player with identical advantages unless the house rules in both places are exactly the same. Obviously, all other factors being equal, you will not win as much playing in a game with very restrictive rules as in one with more liberal options. The following list outlines a few common rule variations and their advantage or disadvantage to the player in percent:

1. Doubling on any number of cards, +.62%
2. Doubling on any three cards, +.2%
3. Doubling allowed after splitting, +.1%
4. Drawing any number of cards to split Aces, +.14%
5. Surrender in shoe games, +.1%
6. Six-card bonus (total of 21 or less), +.17
7. No doubling on 9s or 10s, −.7%
8. Dealer hits soft 17s, −.2%
9. No soft doubling allowed, −.14%
10. No resplitting of pairs, −.05%
11. No hole card (charity and Europe), −.13%

For example, playing at the Vegas Club, which advertises "The Most Liberal '21' Rules in the world," in order to calculate your BS playing gain you would add the percentages from numbers 1, 3, 5, and 6 (plus perhaps

0.1 for resplitting Aces—no specific percentage is given for this beneficial variation) for a total of +1.09%, but subtract number 8. Therefore, your overall BS advantage expectation when playing at Vegas Club would be approximately +.9% (less other minor variables such as the number of decks used, etc.), which means that even without counting cards you would still have some odds with you, slight as they may be.

## Calculating Appropriate Bet Sizes

There is no need to factor in changes to your BS playing advantage every time you go from one casino to another. Minor variations will not affect the calculation of your bet size enough to worry about. The main consideration used by counters to determine their advantage at any given point in the game is the true count (TC), as explained in chapter 6. Professor Peter Griffin has calculated that a player's advantage is the BS gain (as shown above) plus approximately half the TC. Therefore, playing in a casino with rules that provide you an even game, your advantage in percent is always roughly half the TC.

Applying the Kelly Criterion, you can easily determine any proper bet size by multiplying your advantage in percent (i.e., half the TC) times your bankroll. If your bankroll is $1,000 and the TC is +2, then your ideal wager should be $10. Unfortunately, this bet-sizing guide is only recommended for conservative players when the TC is +4 or less, since other factors should also be taken into consideration before deciding upon the amount of your wager. The 2% Rule is one; it is explained in chapter 5.

The smaller the portion of your bankroll that you bet when you have an advantage, the more likely you will end up doubling it instead of losing it. (Many players decide to end sessions once they double their playing stakes; this acts as a signal that they have accomplished a short-term goal.) Various mathematicians have proven that betting a maximum of only 1% of a player's total bankroll even when he has as little as a 2% advantage, results in doubling the bankroll over 98% of the time! (See Richard Epstein's *The Theory of Gambling and Statistical Logic*.) With less than 1% advantage, you will double your hundred-unit bankroll almost five out of every six sessions, betting only one unit per hand. Epstein coined the phrase "minimum boldness" to describe this approach. If this seems hard to believe, consider the following:

Suppose your bankroll totals $1,000 and your game plan is to play until you double it (or lose it all). You decide to bet only when you have a 2% advantage over the house, i.e., when the TC = +4. If you plunk it all down on one hand, your chances of winning (and therefore doubling your bankroll) are only 51%, since the casino will win with these odds 49% of the time. Only two times out of a hundred will you achieve your objective with this bold gesture.

However, if you continually wager only $10 on each hand (i.e., 1% of your bankroll) with this same advantage, you will end up doubling your bankroll over 98% of the time. In other words, for every hundred such sessions, you would lose your entire bankroll (i.e., suffer "gambler's ruin" as described below) only twice. If you divide your bankroll or playing stake into fifty betting units, i.e., $20 a hand, your chances of doubling it falls to slightly over 88%. This is still a good win-rate resulting from the maximum percentage (2%) of one's bankroll that is recommended to be wagered on any one hand, no matter what figure the Kelly Criterion might suggest. (This is the 2% Rule; see chapter 5 for more details.) Although not nearly as exciting, placing the smallest possible bets you are allowed to make (i.e., table minimums) when you have any sort of odds advantage gives you the greatest possible chance of doubling your money while never really risking anything.

More aggressive players choose to follow the Kelly Criterion by regularly making wagers greater than 2% of their bankroll as the TC rises, but they risk ruin far more often. For example, by betting up to 10% of their bankrolls with the same 2% advantage, their chances of doubling them drop to 60%. There are some high-rolling VIPs who habitually bet large sums with apparently no regard to the Kelly Criterion whatsoever. For example, in 1995, Kerry Packer, Australia's richest man, effortlessly won $20 million on a forty-minute blackjack spree in Las Vegas. It should be remembered that, unless he was a skilled counter and was ranging his bets according to the TC, Packer could have lost that amount of money in the same length of time just as easily.

This is precisely the mathematical principle upon which casinos thrive. By letting a small edge grind away at millions of wagers over the years, overwhelming successes are virtually guaranteed. How else could a game like craps, with an advantage of only 1.4%, be such a big moneymaker for the house? As any businessperson can attest, the answer is volume; it is much better to have a small percentage of a lot of money than a large percentage of a little.

## Gambler's Ruin

Observing the 2% Rule mentioned above practically ensures that you will never lose your entire blackjack-playing bankroll. Only those players who place wagers in excess of 2% or play in games where they do not enjoy an advantage will likely experience the gut-wrenching agony of "gambler's ruin," i.e., losing all of their gambling money.

On the following graph, note your approximate chances in percent of experiencing gambler's ruin as opposed to doubling your bankroll, according to the number of betting units and the odds advantages offered in some common games played:

# Chance Of Experiencing Gambler's Ruin

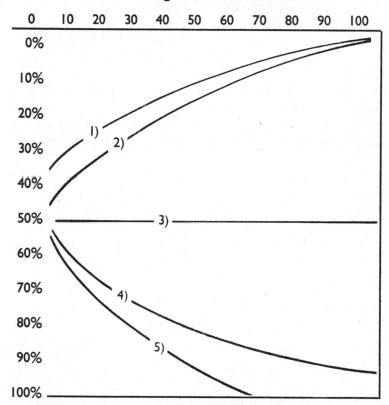

**Betting Units To Be Doubled**

1. The most efficient computer-generated Blackjack counting system using a 1–8 bet range (not humanly possible under casino conditions), +4% advantage.

2. High-low MBS-2 with 1–4 bet range (described in chapters 6 and 7), which has a playing efficiency of about +2.7%.

3. Blackjack's BS alone (single deck, no counting), +.01%.

4. Craps, −1.4%.

5. Roulette, −5.26%.

## More BS Advantages

Following only the BS presented in chapter 3, you will win more, lose less, and sometimes even win instead of losing in the long run, as the following situation illustrates.

When you are holding a pair of 6s versus 4, you will win only 42.5% of the time by standing. The dealer will win 57.5%, which means that your overall losses would be 15%. By splitting your 6s, you increase your win percentage to 51%. Since the dealer's win rate after this split will be 49%, your gain is 2% × 2, because you will have doubled your total amount of money on the table. Therefore, by splitting you turn a losing situation (−15%) into a winning one (+4%), which results in an overall gain of 19%.

BS also insures that you will lose less on certain hands. When you are dealt A,7 versus T, you are stuck with a losing hand no matter how you play it. By standing, your win rate is only 41%, while hitting this soft 18 will beat the dealer's final total just 43% of the time. Standing results in a net loss of 18% (dealer's win rate of 59% minus your 41%), while hitting provides a net loss of only 14%. You will generally lose in this situation, but you will lose less (4% to be exact) by following BS.

## Multiple-parameter Tables

In chapter 6 a number of counting systems are described in which various cards are assigned a value of zero. In the Hi-Low system 7s, 8s, and 9s are ignored. Other systems count Aces as 0 in the running count (RC) but keep track of them separately, since they are too important to ignore. By keeping track of the cards that count zero, however, it is possible to increase the playing efficiency of a counting system by using such information.

In 1975, Professor Peter Griffin devised tables that compensate for ignoring zero-valued cards. For example: On one of Griffin's tables, 9s have an index value of −1, Ace's = −2, and 8s = 0. Therefore, in a single-deck game if a counter noticed that three 9s were seen in the first half deck, he should add −1 to the normal RC, because one extra 9 appeared (beyond the normal distribution expectation). Similarly, if no Aces had appeared, +4 would necessarily be added to the RC (−2 × 2 = −4, which is subtracted from the RC).

Although multiple-parameter tables may be useful for a few professional players who have learned certain counting systems, the additional effort required to keep the necessary side-counts in one's head and adjust the RC accordingly does not justify the tiny gain of only .4% that such tables can provide. They are mentioned here not as an endorsement but merely to inform readers that such sophisticated research has been done and is available to those who might be interested in purchasing it.

# 5

# Money Management

In a sense, everything in this book could rightly be considered "money management," since all of the advice is geared toward increasing winnings and decreasing losses while playing the game of blackjack. Money management in this chapter, however, deals specifically with every aspect of the game other than how to play your cards correctly. In the broadest sense, money management is simply your overall game plan for staying ahead of the casinos financially.

## The Need for Money Management

Proper money management virtually insures that you win more than you lose, regardless of the cards you may receive. There are players who have learned the correct BS as found in chapter 3, mastered the implementation of a practical counting system as suggested in chapter 6, and have the MBS indices found in chapter 7 all firmly entrenched in their minds, but they still fail to make much money from the game. Poor money management is generally responsible; there is far more to blackjack than merely playing your hands correctly. Incorporating smart money management into your game is essential if you want to end up ahead in the long run.

An expression of my late father comes to mind, which is relevant here. Regarding any game his philosophy was "If you don't play to win, you deserve to lose!" Winning at blackjack is very much a matter of attitude, too. You must have the desire to win, know that you can win, and be determined to remain a winner, or you not only will lose, but you should lose. You must be serious about beating this game; the proof is in your hands right now. If you didn't care whether you won or lost you wouldn't be reading this book.

Unless you aspire to be a professional blackjack player, you will likely play the game primarily for entertainment rather than to make huge amounts of money from it. This does not imply, however, that you should not be playing to win. Many players think of their winnings as "the casino's money," and adopt a cavalier attitude toward them. This is exactly how the casinos want you to feel. It's one of the reasons they insist upon selling you chips to use in the first place. Psychologically, chips are not real money—and certainly not your money, since they have the casino's name stamped into them. Nothing could be further from the truth. Always keep in mind that the chips you win represent real dollars in your pocket. They are equivalent to money in the bank—your bank.

Once they are up money from playing blackjack, most people just hand it all back to the casinos again. Instead of this, learn to consciously consider any gains that you make as your money, the same as the stuff in your wallet. You had to risk your hard-earned "folding green" to earn it. It is not "found money" with which you should play recklessly; rather, any amount that you win immediately forms part of your total blackjack bankroll. Guard those little black chips just as you would $100 bills. Learning how to protect them properly is an integral part of money management.

Incorporating the money management advice found on the following pages will establish you firmly as a consistent winner. It is based on scientific and mathematically sound approaches, which few players know and even fewer follow.

## Bankrolls

Determine the size of your entire blackjack-playing bankroll. This sum represents the total amount of money that you are willing to risk over the course of your whole "blackjack-playing casino holiday." Make absolutely certain that your bankroll is an amount that you can honestly afford to lose, just in case you encounter a long stretch of sustained bad luck. After all, anything can happen in the short run, and you don't want your blackjack playing to put additional strain upon finances back home. Each time you make some money, add it to your total bankroll, and watch it grow in a separate account over the years. You will be amazed at how quickly it builds up using good money management techniques.

## Stakes

Take to the casino no more than 20% of your bankroll for use during any one session or playing period. This amount is known as your playing "stake." By physically limiting yourself to only one-fifth of your total bankroll, you are less likely to "chase" the inevitable losses that occur from time to time. Regardless of how bad a single session may be, you will never run the risk of being financially or emotionally devastated by it, since you will have lost only a small portion of your whole blackjack bankroll. A playing stake should be about fifty times the minimum wager you normally make, thereby allowing you to ride out all but the wildest of storms. If you plan to play only at a $2 table, you should bring to the casino no more than $100 as your stake for that session.

## The 2% Rule

Make sure that you never wager more than 2% of your total blackjack bankroll on any one hand, no matter how favorable the playing conditions may appear. If your bankroll is only $500, you should be playing only at the $1 or $2 tables, and at appropriate times ranging your bets up to $10 as a maximum. If your bankroll is $1000, you should never place a single bet of more than $20. At this level of betting, you will probably make less than $10 an hour, but you will be having fun while you learn. Playing with "scared" money (i.e., money that you are afraid of losing) leeches most of the enjoyment from the game.

Resign yourself to the fact that you can't have your financial cake and eat it too. If you decide to play within reasonable safety margins, you cannot expect to make a fortune from blackjack overnight. The good news, however, is that you will never lose much by abiding by the 2% Rule. The average counter's win-rate is only one-and-a-half times his neutral (i.e., minimum) bet per hour, assuming that one can play about fifty hands per hour. Obviously, if you want to make more, you have to risk more. Normally a good player has to play $20 hands for an hour to make $30. At this rate your maximum bets would be $100 or so, which means that you could spare a bankroll of $5,000. In the world of blackjack, as well as in real life, one cannot run with the rabbit *and* hunt with the hounds.

Not much ventured, not much gained; but are you willing to risk $1,000 to make $30 an hour? There's no guarantee it'll be during the next hour, either. The law of large numbers applies here, as outlined in chapter 4. If you play correctly long enough, you will win at least that hourly rate; however, you might lose that much every hour for a day or two before probability theory begins to turn the tide. Test your skills by taking a more conservative approach, especially at first. Play at tables that offer the lowest minimums. You can always increase your neutral wagers as your bankroll builds.

When the count climbs to unexpected heights, it is always tempting for beginning players to "bet a bundle" in order to "make a killing." However, you must remember that even with TC's of 10 or more, there is still a significant chance of losing any particular hand. It is unwise to risk an inappropriate amount of your bankroll on any one hand, simply because of greed. Remember the 2% Rule. Wagering more is over-betting, and you will be courting gambler's ruin, i.e., losing everything. Be satisfied to let your profits build up gradually. Keep in mind that winning blackjack is a slow grind for even the professionals. If you are looking for a get-rich-quick scheme, it is certainly not this game. Remember Epstein's "minimum boldness" approach from chapter 4: Betting smaller amounts will tend to double your playing stakes more often.

Rest assured that whatever the size of your bets, there will always be players who cavalierly risk twice as much on every wager. Swallow any false pride that may tend to stick in your craw, and resist the temptation to wager more than 2% of your bankroll simply because some goof next to you may be flaunting his wealth by shoving out stacks of green or black chips every hand. Know that the main difference between you and him is that tomorrow you will still have your bankroll, no doubt modestly increased, and that you will still be playing and making money from the game. He may never be seen again.

## Game Plans

"If you fail to plan, then plan to fail." Whoever coined this phrase was likely not referring to financial success at blackjack, but nevertheless the truth of the statement applies. Developing a game-playing plan, and sticking to it, is absolutely essential for continued success. Before leaving your hotel room for the casino, decide exactly where, when, and how you will play your next session.

### Where You Will Play

If possible, choose a casino that offers the most favorable playing conditions, all other factors being equal. Conditions are determined by comparing such things as rules variations, the number of decks used, table minimums, number of players usually found at the tables, and even the proximity of the casino to your room.

Try not to play at the same establishment all the time, or even regularly. It doesn't take long for floor people to notice and remember winners. Normally, you can play safely at any casino for short periods of time—say, up to an hour—without drawing undue attention to yourself, especially during personnel shifts.

Choosing the proper table at which to play can be as important a consideration as some rule restrictions. Surveys have shown, and it has been proven mathematically, that you are generally further ahead playing at a table with the lowest minimum, the fewest players, and where there is a slow-dealing, young, pleasant-mannered female dealer. If the rules are the same, choosing a single- or double-deck game over a shoe is more to the player's advantage, as explained in chapter 4. Obviously, you will not often find all of these ideal circumstances available, but you can choose a table where the greatest number of them exist.

Try to sit at the first-base spot (the dealer's extreme left) whenever possible. One reason is that you'll never have to crane your neck around to view all the other hands while counting, since this position offers an unobstructed view of the whole table. You brand yourself as a counter if you deliberately move to see all cards that come into play.

Another good reason to sit at first base is that you'll get better cards when the count is high and you have more money out on the table. For example, if the TC is 3 with two decks left, and there are two other players at your table, eight cards must be dealt before any playing decisions are made. You would get the first and fifth cards, while the third player would get the third and seventh. If all the cards are good ones, i.e., T's and Aces, the count would be negative before the third player received his second card. Better him than you.

This principle applies even more strongly when you're playing a single- or double-deck game, or when there is a full complement of players at the table. Your chances of getting better cards increase when the count is positive, if you are sitting at the first-base spot. This is more important than your increased probability of receiving small cards when the count is negative, since you will have fewer chips on the table during those times, if you decide to play under such adverse conditions at all.

Some blackjack writers advise sitting at the third-base spot instead, since it allows just as good table viewing while also giving the player more time to think about his plays, which should be appreciated by beginning players and experienced counters alike. It is true that third base sees more cards (especially in shoe games, which are dealt up) before having to make any playing decisions. However, this provides only a very small advantage. The few extra cards seen by the third-base player rarely influence the TC enough to justify a change in playing strategy. Getting better starting totals, i.e., by sitting at first base, is more important than playing your hand according to 100% correct MBS.

Pit bosses and other floor people know that counters often tend to sit at the dealer's extreme right. Perhaps the most important reason to avoid third base is that these players are indeed noticed more often. You can do without this arbitrary scrutiny. Whether they choose to stand or hit, third-base players always seem to influence the dealer's third card more directly; therefore, this player attracts attention every time the dealer busts or draws a pat hand. The fact that third base is, consequently, often blamed for a dealer's good pull makes this spot at the table more prominent. A wise player avoids unnecessary attention of any kind.

### When You Will Play

Deciding when to play means more than simply choosing the best time of day. Casinos are generally busiest from eight o'clock in the evening until well after midnight. It is always more difficult to find an empty or one-player table during these hours. Crowded conditions are seldom the best in which to play, unless you are seeking complete anonymity.

Knowing when to play implies knowing when *not* to play. Counters should decide ahead of time just how negative they will allow the TC to become (if at all) before they will refuse to continue playing. Also, if a dealer seems suspicious, is not friendly, or begins hiding cards in games dealt down, it is time to move on before heat from the floor drives you away.

In addition, you may decide to stop playing when one of the following happens: (a) you double your stake, (b) you lose your stake, or (c) you have played continuously for two hours.

*The Stop-loss Limit* Smart players quit playing when they reach what is known as their "stop-loss" limit. The stop-loss limit varies with the individual and the amount won, but it begins as a specific percentage of one's playing stake, generally around a third. For example, if your net loss is equivalent to thirty or so minimum bets (from a playing stake of a hundred units), you are wise to at least change tables, if not exit the casino entirely. After all, you may have encountered a "mechanic" dealer who was cheating you. On the other hand, if you easily double your session's stake, your stop-loss limit would increase to sixty units. Continue playing until you reach your new stop-loss limit, or other factors indicate that it's time to quit. This way you will always be quitting while you are ahead, unless you experience an unusually high number of losses at the start of a session. Otherwise, you keep salting away two-thirds of your winnings indefinitely. Unless you are mentally well disciplined, actually place this two-thirds gain into a not-to-be-touched-under-any-circumstances pocket. In any case, you will never lose more than your original stop-loss limit before pushing away from the table.

Many players fail to realize that the old adage "Never leave a winning streak!" does not mean that one should only depart all tables as a loser. It is extremely important to know when to quit. You feel yourself getting tired, or you begin losing track of the counts, or you find yourself being easily distracted, or you start becoming emotionally involved in the game, or you begin accepting the free alcoholic beverages offered by ever-more-attractive-looking cocktail waitresses—these are all signals that you definitely need to take a break.

Be sure to consciously include when to stop playing in your game plan; otherwise, you may find yourself making foolish decisions at the tables. These will end up costing you money, and you almost certainly will regret them later. There is absolutely no need for you to lose your whole playing stake (i.e., three losing tables in a row at which you reach your stop-loss limit) more often than the laws of probability predict simply because you didn't know enough to quit when you should have.

### How You Will Play

How you decide to play includes such considerations as the size of your neutral wager, the counting system (if any) you will employ, bet-ranging (according to the RC, TC, or flat wagering methods explained in chapter 6), how conservative or aggressive your play will be, or whether you will play every hand regardless of the count. Just as Alice knew, the pleasure derived from a daisy chain sometimes fails to justify the trouble of making it. In other words, simply beating the casinos at blackjack may not be worth the effort involved for some people. There are many factors to consider in determining exactly how you will play the game.

*Partners* Sometimes you may decide to play with partners. This can be a more conservative and financially "risk-free" proposition, since total winnings are divided equally among the participants at the end of each session. One method involves several players sitting at separate uncrowded tables, playing the shoe minimums while patiently counting. Whenever a TC reaches high indices, a roving player is secretly signaled to the table, where he immediately places large bets, often the table maximums. This way, the regular players at the tables do not betray themselves as counters by ranging their own bets too dramatically, if at all. The big wagers are usually accepted by the dealers and floor people without suspicion, because there is no way that the "big" player could have been counting, having just approached the table.

Problems can arise when playing with partners, however, and this practice is not recommended for nonprofessionals. (See Ken Uston's *The Big Player.*) On the other hand, if you know fellow counters that you can trust, team play is a good way to spare yourselves the wild fluctuations often experienced in blackjack. By playing separately during the session, each player can have access to a larger maximum bet (i.e., 2% of your combined bankrolls) and therefore enjoy the advantage of this extra leverage whenever conditions may warrant.

Pick the style of play (conservative, aggressive, or somewhere in between) that is best suited to a particular casino, or simply your individual preference. Make sure that you feel comfortable playing whatever method you choose to employ. Carefully consider and decide upon what sort of play you will use before you arrive in the casino. There is more than enough to think about once you are at the table; you don't need the additional pressure at that time of deciding which playing style you will adopt.

*Conservative Style* The following represents how a very conservative player might decide to play: Making sure the casino allowed doubling on any two cards even after splitting, and surrender was available, he might decide to play only in double-deck games where the dealers stand on all 17s. Never playing under negative or neutral counts, he would place a minimum wager (no more than $2) only if the TC were +3 or better, and increase subsequent bets upward $1 for each odd number the TC rose above 3. His betting range would never exceed four units (or 1% of his bankroll), no matter how high the TC rose. While making sure there was seldom more than one other player at the table (never more than two), always sitting at the first-base spot, and playing his hands according to proper MBS only, this type of overcautious player would likely not get to play more than a half-dozen hands per hour, and therefore could not expect to win much. However, there is virtually no chance of his losing money playing this way. A conservative-style player must be content with correspondingly modest winnings, but he has virtually taken the gamble out of the game.

*Wonging* Although not as conservative as the above hypothetical individual, Stanford Wong practiced a mildly conservative approach, by playing only in positive games. He would stand behind tables while counting the cards until the count turned positive. Only then would he slide in a medium-sized bet. He would continue to play there as long as the count remained steady or increased, raising his bets accordingly, but he would immediately leave the table once the count dropped to zero. This "in and out" style of play, which involves a lot of back-counting from behind the tables, has come to be known as "Wonging," after the master blackjack player-writer who originated it. Wonging is physically exhausting, because you are on your feet so much; however, never playing a single hand under negative conditions is often a profitable undertaking that is worth the effort. Unfortunately, more and more casinos are implementing "no midshoe entry" policies to defeat the practice of Wonging.

It is not always possible for conservative players to play safely in a given casino at any specific time. For example, if table minimums are too high, all the tables are crowded, and only eight-deck shoe games are offered, a conservative player would be wiser not to play at all under such conditions. Even an experienced counter could not be guaranteed enough profit to justify his time in such a game. A truly conservative player would scout out more favorable playing conditions.

*Aggressive Style* Aggressive players' winnings fluctuate more, but they will generally make more money in the long run since they play more hands per hour. Aggressive players are not as concerned about minor rule variations. They realize that they will not necessarily make money every time they play. Nevertheless, they do know that by playing a larger number of hands when they have an advantage (and consequently they have more chips on the table), abiding by the appropriate MBS, and ranging their bets more widely (according to the Aggressive TC Wagering Chart from chapter 6), more significant net winnings will certainly accrue to them over time.

The truly aggressive blackjack player is more of a gambler in the traditional sense of the word, since he is comfortable not winning every hand, every session, every day, or even every trip. Although he risks much larger sums of money, he normally takes home much more than the conservative player. The aggressive style is not to be confused with foolhardy play. A competent and prudent player can choose to play aggressively just as well as conservatively. An aggressive player is bolder in his approach to the game, primarily regarding the size and range of bets, but he must also be psychologically able to bear the inevitable "ups and downs" that accompany this type of ride. The larger benefits that fall to these often flamboyant players are their just desserts. To them, the financial roller coaster they experience is definitely worth more than the price of the ticket.

## Comps

"A dollar saved is a dollar earned!" This old saw is basically true, so be sure to take full advantage of casino complimentaries, known simply as "comps." You may as well get your share of free meals, accommodation, show tickets, "match-play" coupons, etc., which are generally available to all casino patrons. Every dollar you save this way can rightly be considered part of your blackjack winnings, as long as you would have purchased these goods or services anyway.

By giving away comps, the casino hopes to entice players to continue playing at that establishment rather than moving on to another. Comps are handed out more easily and frequently where there is a greater selection of casinos from which players may choose. These playing "perks" are easier to obtain in the Las Vegas area, where about fifty casinos are all competing for your gaming dollar. In Vegas, three or four hours of uninterrupted play at a $5 table is often enough to earn you a dinner for two at one of their famous all-you-can-eat buffets. At the other extreme, the Atlantis (near Nassau, in the Bahamas) is extremely reluctant to reward its small-time players with any comps whatsoever. This is probably because the Atlantis is the only casino on the island. There you must play for at least four hours a day with bets of more than $25 a hand in order to receive the slightest comp of any kind.

"Squeaky wheels get the grease." Normally, you have to ask for comps no matter where you play, other than the free drinks offered to all players. "High rollers" who normally wager thousands of dollars a hand often receive substantial comps even without requesting them. Comps are a matter of intense prestige among some players. By requesting a pit boss to "rate" your play, you are, in effect, asking him for potential comps. He will then note the amount of your average bet and how long you play, in order to determine exactly what value of comp you are entitled to receive. Asking to have your play rated in order to gain comps immediately draws attention to yourself. This should be avoided until you are confident that you can completely disguise your counting, or unless you are simply adhering to flat betting and BS alone. Wonging around behind the tables, jumping in and out of games as the TC varies, will never gain you any comps.

In awarding comps, some casinos also take into account the amount of money you win or lose, but this is done rarely, because it is too difficult for them to monitor accurately. I am reminded of a relevant incident that happened a few years ago while I was playing the double-deck games at the Mirage, Las Vegas. I had purchased several hundred dollars worth of chips over the course of maybe an hour, even though I was up a fair bit. (Continually buying more chips labels you as a loser, and secreting them away in your pocket is an easy way to hide the fact that you are actually winning.) I knew that one pit boss in particular had seen me "buy in" more than once, since dealers have to call it to their attention when changing large bills. The next time he came by, I asked innocently, "How much do I have to lose here before I can get a free buffet for me and the wife?" I had only a few red chips on the table in front of me, so he likely assumed that I had lost $300 or $400 there. Without saying a word, he wrote me up the comp immediately. My wife was so embarrassed when she found out how I obtained our free meal that evening, she accused me of being no better than a beggar. I saw her point and have not hustled comps like this since, but the fact remains that had I not asked we would not have received this little blackjack-playing bonus.

## Coupons

The simplest form of comp and the most prevalent is the "match-play" coupon. In one form or another almost every casino offers this sort of incentive for players to belly up to the blackjack tables. Match-play coupons generally come in denominations of $2 to $10 and are obtained from casino promotion booths or from their registration desks. They are often found in "fun books" along with all kinds of discount coupons. Match-play coupons should be considered equivalent to "free casino money." Using them will always overcome the highest blackjack house advantages—even for noncounters. Here's how they work:

In order to use a match-play coupon, simply slide it under your bet. At a $10 minimum table you are often allowed to play a $5 coupon under one red chip in order to make up the minimum wager. If you lose the hand, the coupon is taken along with your $5 chip, but if the hand is a winner, you are paid off as if you had bet the whole amount in casino chips. Each coupon can be used only once. You may as well use coupons to bring your wagers up to the amount you would be betting anyway. In other words, if the TC warrants a $20 bet, playing a $10 coupon under two reds instead of using entirely your own chips makes perfect sense. Using the coupons in addition to your normal wagers, however, would be equivalent to overbetting.

There are two good reasons for using coupons whenever you possibly can. First, they represent free playing chips. If you are not counting cards, $50 worth of match-plays will net you $25 even if you are playing by BS alone, since you can expect to win at least half of your hands on the average. Using the coupons and playing a conservative MBS is virtually a certain way of winning money every session.

Another good reason to use match-play coupons is that they are usually associated with unknowledgeable, beginning players; therefore, you will more likely seem to present no threat to the casino whenever you use them. If you look like a novice, the pit bosses will be less inclined to view you as the danger to casino coffers that you actually are.

Remember that you are playing blackjack primarily to make money from the game, not to get a few free dinners and shows. Be careful that you don't start focusing upon the "something-for-nothing" idea instead of playing blackjack optimally. It would obviously detract from your making any really substantial gains. But, on those days that you plan to sit at a table for a few hours at a time, you are selling yourself short if you don't profit from some of these extra bonuses offered by the casino, regardless of how much money you win without them.

## Junkets

"Junkets" are a type of casino comp that is less common these days but is still worth considering, especially if you plan to take a blackjack-playing holiday somewhere anyway. Junkets consist of groups of people who all agree to risk at least a minimum specified daily amount of money at a particular casino. Their return airfare and accommodation at this casino are provided "free of charge" by the casino management at the end of the excursion. The justification of such a good comp lies in the fact that most unskilled players lose far more than the comps actually cost the casino.

Every junket is different. Some require substantial deposits, which are nonrefundable if a player fails to meet all of the terms of the junket contract. Others have such high daily playing minimums that you would have virtually no available time outside the specified casino, especially if you were to play strictly within your means using proper money management. (Naturally, the casinos want you to wager more than 2% of your bankroll on each hand, because you will more likely achieve "gambler's ruin" that way—i.e., lose your whole bankroll, and then some.)

Being a good blackjack player, however, you can expect to rarely lose money on a junket. Even without counting, you often break even (or slightly better) by simply following correct BS and careful money management techniques. The main drawback is that you are restricted to playing in only one casino, and therefore subject to possibly undesirable playing conditions, e.g., crowded tables or table minimums as high as $25 a hand. Junkets to casinos that have poor rules variations can end up costing even skilled counters more than the comp is worth. Be sure to check out all such relevant factors before automatically signing up to go on the next junket you hear about. (For more about a typical junket, see chapter 15 of Adrian Waller's *The Gamblers*.)

## Record Keeping

Keep a complete and accurate record of all your blackjack sessions. Jot down not only how much you win or lose but also all of the playing conditions encountered, from rule variations to suspicious floor personnel. This information is helpful in updating your current bankroll as well as determining your game plans for future sessions.

Without good documentation it is too easy to lose track of your actual financial position. Players who do not make the effort to write down exactly where they stand daily tend to exaggerate their wins and diminish their losses over time, due primarily to fuzzy recollection rather than deliberate fabrication. As with life in general, it is easier to remember the good times and to forget the bad. Too often, losses from other casino games such as roulette or craps that one plays while on blackjack breaks get unfairly attributed to blackjack by players who keep poor records.

Just watching the black-and-white evidence of your cumulative bankroll increasing over the years is very satisfying in itself. Reviewing past successful playing records can certainly help you through the depression and self-doubts that tend to follow losing sessions. At these times it is especially comforting to note how your total winnings have compounded to date, thereby leaving you confident and eager for your next visit to the tables.

## Casino Credit

Most casinos are happy to provide you with a "line of credit" for any amount you wish, as long as you have enough money in your bank back home to cover it. There is no fee for this service, and it can usually be in place within twenty-four hours after filling out the application. There are a few advantages to using lines of credit, but it is not generally advisable for the vast majority of players.

Since there are no charges for setting up a line of credit in a casino, you are further ahead taking advantage of one rather than obtaining a credit card advance. Card advances generally cost you an up-front fee, if obtained at a casino, plus you pay interest on them from day one. Major banks normally provide credit card advances without charging any additional fees themselves, but you still cannot avoid paying the exorbitant interest rates on the total amount advanced.

If you plan to be wagering large sums of money in the casino, it is safer to have a line of credit established. This way you can avoid carrying around a big roll of $100 bills; crowded casinos represent ideal environments for skilled pickpockets. Once your individual credit system is set up, you can sit down at any table and request a "marker" for whatever amount you wish—up to your established limit. The marker is just an IOU slip, which you sign when receiving your chips. After you have finished playing, you can pay off your marker before leaving the table, and walk away with just your winnings. If you are mugged on the way to your hotel room, at least you won't lose your whole bankroll.

Another reason for you "high rollers" to use casino credit involves your taking advantage of more substantial comps. Each time you take or pay off a marker, the transaction is recorded on a central credit information sheet. Knowing the size and frequency of all the playing markers you use helps casino managers more easily determine what your appropriate comps should be.

Keep in mind that using any casino credit system is neither necessary nor advisable for most players. There are five main drawbacks that you should consider carefully before filling out such an application:

1. Asking for markers always draws undue attention to yourself and your play; being more conspicuous, you are apt to be labeled a winner much more readily.
2. After losing a stake, it is all too easy to obtain another stack of chips on credit, and thereby continue playing, against your better judgment and game plan.
3. It is impossible to remain anonymous. Your complete financial history, as well as personal information, is often made known to the casino through your credit application.
4. Having a line of credit tends to limit your play to that particular casino, when much better playing conditions may be available elsewhere. Unless you plan to establish lines of credit in every casino you play, it is seldom worth the effort.
5. There is always the risk of having your whole account "frozen," including winnings that you may have deposited, if the casino ever suspects you of being a counter (see Ken Uston's *The Big Player*).

## Not Getting Barred

No money management knowledge can possibly help one iota if you are not allowed to actually play the game. Money management becomes as utterly useless as your advanced playing skills if and when you are barred from the casinos. Therefore, the most important aspect of your blackjack money management technique may very well lie in not being detected as a counter, nor even as a consistent winner.

## Do's and Don'ts

The following DO and DON'T lists will help you avoid arousing the suspicion of eagle-eyed pit bosses and conscientious dealers, thereby allowing you to stay in the game and ply your skills:

| | |
|---|---|
| DO stash chips away in a pocket or purse surreptitiously, especially when winning. | DON'T ever use a betting range of more than ten units, no matter how good the count may be. |

DO range your wagers up or down gradually.

DO try to appear relaxed or mildly amused, like most people being "entertained" while on holiday.

DO bet the minimums when getting "heat" from a floor person.

DO just be yourself, basically, since it's the easiest act to maintain convincingly.

DO confirm soft-hand totals with the dealer from time to time, in order to label yourself more of a novice.

DO change tables, pits, and even casinos frequently, to avoid becoming a "fixture."

DO immediately leave the casino if you feel that you are under close scrutiny or suspicion.

DO feel free to play more aggressively as your trip nears its end, in other words, don't worry so much about being barred if you won't be around much longer anyway.

DON'T play too quickly or always seem certain of the correct plays.

DON'T be unsociable, but don't be talkative or overly friendly either.

DON'T dress conspicuously or flash expensive jewelery.

DON'T make larger bets only near the end of the shoe.

DON'T obviously pull back a large wager and replace it with the minimum, just because the dealer decides to shuffle.

DON'T insist upon seeing every card even though you might have to crane your neck to do it.

DON'T always leave a table immediately after it fills up, then proceed to sit at an empty or single-player table nearby.

DON'T bet more than the TC justifies, merely in an attempt to divert possible pit-boss suspicion.

DON'T play too intensely, seem consumed in mental activity, or move your lips while counting.

## Counting on Cruises

It has been my experience that cruise ships are generally oblivious to counters. I have been on several of these floating resorts that have made no attempt whatsoever to discourage blatant card-casers. I have often stood around the tables, jumping in and out of games with bets of any size, or simply asking to be dealt out for a hand or two when the counts have dropped below zero—all without drawing any heat whatsoever from floor personnel.

I recall once noticing a reasonably big winner who was obviously counting the cards, playing head to head with a dealer at a $25 table. He was using correct BS, simply ranging his betting units without exception in direct proportion to the TC, and wagering the minimum whenever it went to zero or below. I had never before (nor have I since) seen such unabashed card-casing audacity. With the pit boss smiling and watching the whole thing, I was truly amazed at his overt boldness. It crossed my mind that I could be witnessing a skimming operation in progress.

Finally, when the TC climbed to +10 near the end of the shoe, I casually slipped a single green chip into the empty box at first base. The counter immediately became quite indignant and asked me if I would mind waiting for the next shoe. Playing dumb, I asked, "Why?" He then protested that he was on a "hot streak," and if I came into the game now it could throw off his luck. Innocently, I looked over to the pit boss and asked her if this was a private table, or if anyone could play here. She explained that the guy wanted the remaining cards in the shoe all for himself. "So, I have to play at another table?" I persisted. "No, it's entirely up to you, sir. It's just that you might get some of the cards that this gentleman was counting on," she replied. Those were her very words! In the end, I played the box anyway, in spite of the man's protestations, and pushed with a 20, while he lost two black chips with a 19. I think we both pushed again with 20s before the shuffle. In any case, the poor guy was so infuriated that I had "stolen his cards," he stormed away, leaving me with the table all to myself. Unfortunately, I couldn't continue to enjoy such ideal counting conditions, because the table minimum was too high for me at that time. The pit boss must have known that the other guy was a counter, but I doubt if she suspected me in the least. Apparently, it would not have made the slightest bit of difference to her anyway.

The point of this anecdote is that cruise ship personnel often appear either to be totally ignorant of telltale counting traits or to be disregarding them completely. Since the former is highly unlikely, they have probably been instructed to do the latter. General surveillance on shipboard is usually minimal or nonexistent. Although a few of the larger ships have two-way mirrors through which casino personnel can watch the action, I know of none at present that have hidden cameras, as most land-based operations do. Onboard casinos are generally too small to warrant such an expense.

Cruise lines can afford to ignore counters for a variety of reasons. Their somewhat restrictive rules are usually enough to protect them. Poor playing conditions such as very narrow table limits (some as poor as $25 to $200), dealers hitting soft 17s, not offering the surrender option, using only shoes with shallowly placed shuffle-cards, allowing just one extra split on any pair, and ensuring crowded tables by restricting the hours that the casino is open are usually enough protective measures to ward off the serious or professional blackjack players. After all, a conscientious counter would not want to risk being barred from the only action available; then he would have nothing to do for the rest of the cruise but eat and lie in the sun like the other passengers. In Vegas or Atlantic City, if you happen to be barred, there are always dozens of other good places to practice your skills. Not so when trapped aboard a ship. And why spend money for a cruise anyway, if your primary purpose is to make money? (Unless your significant other or spouse, like mine, enjoys the fine dining, the security, the exotic ports of call, etc.)

To summarize, most cruise companies are far more interested in keeping their passengers happy and entertained, in order to win their repeat business, than they are in losing a few dollars to the odd card-sharp now and then.

## The Psychology of Blackjack

There are several interesting books about the psychology of gambling. At least one professor of psychology has theorized that there is a stronger human motive toward "play" than there is toward "work." If this is true, then the game of blackjack offers the promise of complete fulfillment in this sense, since it is certainly a form of adult play. Many psychologists have written about the "altered state of consciousness" that gambling in general tends to produce, but only blackjack gives the player that additional feeling of being in complete control of his own destiny at the same time.

In chapter 2, the playing decisions flowchart illustrates the high degree of player input required to resolve blackjack hands. No other casino game demands such a level of player involvement. The mouthwatering (albeit subconscious) carrot dangled in front of blackjack players nowadays is simply this: Through skillful play, you may never need to work again. This feeling of autonomy, coupled with the knowledge that the game can be beaten, incessantly tantalizes baby boomers and yuppies alike. And it could partially explain the tremendous growth in the blackjack industry, which has been especially evident over the last ten years.

There is no doubt that gambling can produce "highs," or peak experiences, like nothing else. This accounts for its well-known addictive qualities. While in almost mystical states, players are often transported into fantasy worlds. There they can prove to themselves their "true worth," and consequently affirm their own existence. ("I play, therefore I am!"—with apologies to Descartes.) This may sound too far-fetched to some readers, but please, do not dare dismiss the profound and complex influence that gambling has upon the human psyche.

Many claim that they play blackjack "for the fun of it" and not necessarily to win money. This must be true, since it has been shown that less than 1% of the gambling public actually beats this casino game in the long run. Not being able to articulate the real reasons that they are attracted to the game, others say that, win or lose, just playing simply makes them feel more "alive."

Blackjack definitely arouses appropriate emotional responses: hope, excitement, euphoria; and/or disappointment, frustration, and regret—to name just a few. When we win, our self-esteem swells because we had the courage to risk and the skill to make the right decisions. We feel omnipotent, almost like "heroes." When we lose, however, we then have the opportunity to silently vent our subliminal anger, hostility, and aggression upon the dealer and cards specifically and the casino and our hard-knock life in general. In either case we are definitely involved. Someone once said, "The most exciting thing about playing blackjack is winning; the second most exciting thing is losing."

If you expect to be a long-term winner playing blackjack, you should be aware of the powerful lure such altered states of consciousness can have upon your mind. You must develop a game plan and follow it religiously. Otherwise, instead of your controlling the game, the game will end up controlling you. Blackjack has taken virtual reality to a higher level than any computer-generated program can. Be constantly vigilant, and remind yourself that you are playing primarily to make money and not merely to have fun in these lavish "fantasy environments" so generously provided by the casinos.

## The Luck/Chance Quandary

Not understanding the difference between "luck" and "chance" has cost gamblers plenty over the years. Part of the problem lies in semantics, while part comes from just plain ignorance. When the French say, *"Bonne chance!"* they really mean "Good luck!" Luck and chance refer to fortune and probability respectively. Luck is not a commodity that everyone receives at birth, nor should you expect $x$ amount of good luck during your lifetime. Players who trust providence to make them winners at blackjack are simply too lazy to learn how to win for themselves, i.e., by playing with the mathematically proven odds in their favor. They are truly gamblers. Blackjack is partially a game of chance, since luck is always a factor, but when enough skill is applied it is possible to remove the "gambling" perspective from blackjack's big picture entirely.

Cicero once said, "Probabilities direct the conduct of a wise man." Just because you play, for example, using the MBS described in chapter 7 correctly, does not guarantee that you will not lose; it simply means that you will probably win. The widespread misconception that luck will necessarily change (i.e., that after a series of losses one is somehow "due" for a series of wins) has resulted in much player chagrin (see myth 6 in chapter 4). Probability theory clearly indicates that a trend is just as apt to continue as to reverse; therefore, a player's bad luck can follow him for a lifetime. Any blackjack player's time at the tables must be considered only short-term with respect to the infinite probability curve. It is certainly "unlucky" for you whenever you lose a session, especially after playing every hand optimally, but your fortune will not change because of luck or the law of averages intervening. Only if the odds are with you will your bad luck eventually turn to good.

Never depend upon Lady Luck. She is an untrustworthy old

acquaintance at best. As Machiavelli pointed out, "He who holds the least to fortune is in the strongest position." (Was he plagiarizing Cicero?) Griffith K. Owens, who wrote and played under his better-known pseudonym of Lawrence Revere, always maintained that a good blackjack player never guesses, he *knows*. Knowledge of the game and the skillful use of MBS advice generated from the results of millions of hands are your only reliable cohorts. Luck is fictitious; computer-based statistical research is factual. The ancient Greeks had a saying worth remembering, "Good luck is the reward of the skillful." Believe this, and financial success will surely accompany your blackjack playing for the rest of your life.

## The Macho Mentality

The lure of playing beyond one's limits is sometimes difficult to ignore. Some blackjack players feel a sense of superiority when they are placing the highest wagers at a table. Others feel that they have a leg up on weaker players whenever they deign to explain some aspect of the game to them. Some are too proud to admit that they can't count and play as fast as the dealer can deliver the cards, and consequently end up playing an inferior game. These are all forms of a losing "macho" mentality.

It is more exciting to bet a black chip rather than a red one; there is no doubt about that. But if you do so, unless your blackjack bankroll is at least $5,000 and the TC is good, you are playing with your emotions instead of with the odds (see the TC wagering guide in chapter 6). Players who regularly overbet and thus play somewhere out there beyond their safe depth are easily recognized. They are apt to be more concerned with who's watching them play than with whether they're winning. They typically care more about the virile "he-man" image that they are valiantly trying to project to other players at the table or to specific casino personnel. Tragically, they too often are using money that they cannot really afford to lose. One should feel a little pity for these macho-blackjack-masochists.

If you find yourself being rushed into making playing decisions by a dealer, don't let foolish pride compromise your ability to win. Who can play faster is not the issue, so there is no reason to be drawn into this silly type of competition. Remember that the dealer is at your disposal, like an employee; you have nothing you need to prove to her. You are there to make money, not to engage in battles of one-upmanship with strangers who are merely showing how efficiently they can do their job.

It is a simple matter to slow down a dealer. She cannot pass you by until receiving a stand signal. Control the pace of the game from the start by examining your cards carefully and deliberately, even if you know at a glance what you are going to do. Give yourself time to calculate the TC and recall relevant MBS plays. Then be clear and decisive with your hand signals, thereby forcing the dealer to conform to your playing rate. There is no need to overdo it by slowing the game to a crawl just to prove who's really the boss, especially if there are other players at your table.

Whatever you do, don't fall prey to this macho-type battle between yourself and the dealer. If your ego can stand the beating, it's much better to appear as a novice player who wins, rather than a "good" player who doesn't. Be content to let your financial successes soothe your injured pride, and leave the macho posturing for the losers to practice.

## The Gravy Train

Remember that implementing good money management skills and learning how to play optimally only gets you halfway to where you want to go. The other part of your ticket consists of successfully hiding your acquired knowledge and skills, because the casinos will not hesitate to bar you from playing once they realize you can beat them. If you can disguise the fact that you are actually an expert, however, there is no limit to how far you can journey on the Blackjack Express.

# 6

# Counting Systems

There are almost as many "systems" for playing the game of blackjack as there are blackjack players themselves. Some use strictly their "gut feelings" to govern their play; I dub them "VIP's," which stands for Viscerally Influenced Players. Some VIP's employ progressive bet-ranging schemes as well as strictly intuition. Other players go by "mimic the dealer" or "never bust" strategies, while still others use a bit of anything and everything according to how their luck happens to be holding up at any given moment.

Unfortunately for all these optimistic, well-intentioned players, absolutely none of their systems or playing strategies can make them money in the long run, as long as the casino has even the slightest percentage overall odds advantage. As shown in Myth 3 of chapter 4, all the intricate bet-ranging systems and get-rich-quick schemes in the world won't help the unskilled blackjack player one iota more than rubbing the rabbit's foot he carries around in his pocket. Don't be too quick to laugh at this idea; many players believe wholeheartedly in one form of superstition or another, and they take their old wives' tales very seriously.

The bottom line is this: The only way you are going to beat the game of blackjack is to play it so that the overall odds are in your favor. Explaining how this can be accomplished is the purpose of this chapter.

## The Need

Even though you may play all of your blackjack hands correctly, i.e., according to the BS presented in chapter 3, you will never make much money in the long haul regardless of the liberality of casino rules. BS combined with all of the 101 tips offered in chapter 8, plus all of the other playing and money management advice given throughout these pages, provides you with only a tiny percentage advantage if you do not also track the cards and play your hands accordingly.

Although some days you will win a few hundred dollars easily using BS alone, other times you are just as apt to lose almost as much. You will definitely enjoy an edge over many casinos even without counting cards, but you can never hope to reap all of the extraordinary successes that can accrue from card-casing without learning to count for yourself.

If you are content with modest long-term winnings and play blackjack primarily for the fun of it, to socialize with friends over free drinks or merely to soak up the exciting ambiance of the casino, then you don't need to count cards at all. It should be clearly understood that playing BS without a counting system does little more than bring you even with the house, but this is good enough for some players.

If you really hate losing, however, or you want to exercise a truly significant advantage over the casinos whenever you play, you will necessarily have to select a practical counting system and spend several days learning to implement it properly. Your future profits will be in direct proportion to the effort you put into mastering the various skills and knowledge of the professional counter.

## What Counting Systems Do

Using a counting system that gives you only 3% advantage is more than enough to make you a big winner as long as you play a sufficient number of hands. After all, European roulette has a house advantage of only 2.6% or less, and craps is as low as 1.4%! If such a small edge can make the casinos rich from these games, it can obviously do the same for you from playing blackjack. The secret is to play a large number of hands when the odds are with you, thereby giving the laws of probability an opportunity to kick in.

All legitimate counting systems accomplish four goals:

1. They indicate who has the odds advantage before each deal, allowing you to decide whether or not to play.
2. They determine how much of an edge exists, one way or the other, so that you can range your wagers appropriately.
3. They make the correct decisions about your insurance options easier to calculate.
4. They suggest how much you need to change your BS playing, if at all.

## Why Counting Systems Work

Only in blackjack do the cards have what can rightly be considered a kind of "memory." One type of card is not just as likely as any other to appear next. Almost a third of every deck consists of a single card—the 10-valued card. Whether they are "painted" cards (Jacks, Queens, and Kings) or regular 10s, they are all equivalent members of this group labeled "T" for 10. Fortunately, these most abundant cards are also the most valuable to the player. To cite an obvious example, they are essential in the formation of blackjacks. Although there is far more chance that a non-T will be dealt first from a freshly shuffled deck, the odds that a T will appear rather than any *other* card are always much greater. This is true because the T's predominate; there are simply so many more of them than anything else—four times as many, in fact. In this sense, the deck always "remembers" to favor the T's whenever possible.

This is not the only reason that the deck in a blackjack game may be viewed as having its own sort of memory. As individual cards are brought into play during the course of a game, the composition of the remaining deck changes. Those spent cards are no longer part of the available pool; therefore, the normal distribution within the deck is upset. Cards about to appear next must "remember" to take this inequality of access into account and conform to the new set of probabilities that happens to apply at any particular moment during the game.

Think about this hypothetical situation: You are playing a six-deck shoe game, one-on-one with the dealer, and have been carefully keeping track of all the cards as they are used up during play. Unlikely as it may be, assume that you could now know for a fact that only 8s remain to be dealt. This means that any other cards are not just unlikely to appear before the next shuffle, they absolutely cannot be drawn from the remaining shoe. Under these circumstances, how much should you bet on your next hand?

It is important that you take a second to think about this imaginary but unique situation, because it illustrates a counter's perspective on the game very well. Knowing how much to bet on the next hand, according to the odds of winning or losing, represents one of the card-caser's biggest advantages. (The other main part of a counter's edge lies in the knowledge of how best to play every hand optimally, according to the MBS as presented in chapter 7.) So, have you decided how much to wager in this scenario? The answer, of course, is "Bet the ranch!" You can't possibly lose, unless you absentmindedly hit your original two-card total of 16.

Although it is an extremely atypical example, the above no-lose situation could never come about in any other casino game, even hypothetically. Other games all enjoy their various fixed percentage advantages over the player for every wager made. Therefore, such an opportunity could not possibly present itself. It illustrates how only blackjack can be beaten through astute observation of which cards have already been played and the implementation of more appropriate playing decisions based upon that information. Depending upon which cards are left to be dealt to the player(s) and dealer, sometimes the odds favor the house, sometimes they are completely neutral, but sometimes they favor the player! Herein lies the big distinction for blackjack, and *vive la différence!* Only an experienced counter, however, knows before any given deal exactly where the advantage lies.

## How Counting Systems Work

When it is impossible that certain cards be dealt to you, the original composition or "balance" of the full deck(s) is obviously skewed. A particular card can no longer appear completely at random. This situation could easily happen, for example, if you were to observe that all four Aces had already been used up in a single-deck game. Your chances of being dealt a blackjack before the cards were shuffled again would be zero. Not an ideal situation, of course. Also, you could not receive any soft hands, which normally represent big gains for the player (they gravitate toward winning totals about 65% of the time). Nor could you hope to split Aces, your most advantageous of all possible splits.

With the Aces gone, the player is at nearly a 3% disadvantage in a single-deck game, as seen in Thorp's table, chapter 4.

Although obviously possessing no intelligence per se, the deck in the above example nevertheless must "remember" that the Aces are no longer available and that none can appear before the next shuffle. If you had noted this fact, you would have a definite advantage over other players who were not watching the cards as carefully. You would, therefore, likely decide to place a smaller than usual bet for your next hand, because of this "privileged" information concerning the lesser likelihood of your winning with a blackjack. Another example of the counter's edge over the casino, this kind of thinking represents one of the cornerstones of all counting systems, i.e., risking less when the odds of winning are obviously reduced.

At the other extreme, if you were to note that no Aces had been seen in a game, and the last hand before the shuffle was about to be dealt, you would be wise to increase your wager at that point, since your odds of getting a blackjack on the next hand would be much greater than immediately after a shuffle. The dealer, too, will have the same increased likelihood of a blackjack, but your blackjack pays you 3 to 2, while his wins only even money; therefore, you would generally wind up ahead under such circumstances. All other factors being equal, counters wager in a similar fashion; they place larger bets when the probability of winning is greater.

Suppose that the first ten cards that come out in a single-deck game were all painted. The chance that the very next card to be dealt would also be a face card is not as good as it was originally, since the number of available T's is now very much depleted. This doesn't necessarily mean that a face card could not appear immediately, just that it probably would not. Similarly, if you saw that the first ten cards were all of low rank, the odds would be diminished that the very next card to appear would also be a small one. Since every deck is composed of a finite number of cards of each rank, the probability of any particular card being dealt at any specific time is entirely dependent upon which cards still remain to be chosen from the available pool.

Bet more when your chances of winning are greater, and less (or nothing at all) when the odds favor the casino. This is the counter's credo. The more favorable your odds, the more money you can justifiably risk. This may sound like obvious advice, and it is certainly an ideal strategy, but the question now is this: How can even a counter know where the advantage lies, and how great it is, all the time? The answer: by simply developing accurate card-tracking abilities, which are well within the grasp of every motivated individual.

Playing skill, and only skill, forces the house to relinquish its edge in the game of blackjack. Remembering which cards appear during the course of normal play, adjusting the size of your bets up or down according to your advantage, and playing your hands in the best possible manner—these are the skills of a counter. They can make virtually anyone a big winner. With practice, you too can be a participating member of this elite and very successful group.

"Counting" or "tracking" or "casing" all refer to methods by which one takes note of the cards as they are used up in a game. Hopefully, you now possess an inkling of how a counter makes use of this data to calculate the relative player advantage (or disadvantage) that exists at any given time during the game. This "extra" information allows the card-tracker to better determine the appropriate size of his next bet and to range it accordingly. If you are playing at a $2 minimum table, for example, you can normally change your bets up and down between $2 and $10 in direct proportion to the advantage you enjoy, without drawing undue attention from the dealer or floor personnel. The larger the unit bets, however, the more careful you have to be in ranging your wagers.

Depending upon which cards have already been exposed during the game, a counter may also wish to modify BS plays, since the probability of drawing certain cards is no longer completely random. Similarly, the card-counting player exploits the use of all proposition bets (i.e., surrender, doubling, splitting, and insurance) to full advantage in order to make the overall odds lean even more significantly in his favor. In this way, a card-counting system rewards the tracker's skill by providing the essential data necessary to increase winning opportunities.

## Counting Systems

### Thorp's Five-count Strategy

In the early 1960s, with the help of powerful computers, Edward Thorp proved conclusively that the removal of all four 5s from single-deck play resulted in the player's advantage over the dealer increasing by 3.6%. As a strategy for single-deck play, he suggested that players take note of how many 5s remained to be dealt in order to range their bets more relevantly. Using BS until all four 5s came out of the deck, a player following this simple "Five-count" strategy enjoyed an average edge of almost 3%. Even though all the 5s were rarely used up early in any game, and the player's small bets won less than normal BS expectations, the player could still achieve and maintain a significant advantage over the dealer by using this strategy. This was the first simple counting system that worked, and it is just as effective today.

Thorp suggested playing a modified BS when none of the 5s are available to be dealt. The relevant changes include standing with 12 versus all dealer stiff cards, with 15 versus 9 and 10, and with three or more cards totaling 16 versus a 7 or 8. Several other MBS plays were recommended, and the interested reader may study them all at leisure in the second edition of *Beat the Dealer,* page 49.

Speaking about his Five-count strategy, Thorp pointed out, "One skilled player whom I know asserts that he can play 350 hands per hour when playing head on. Betting from $1 to $500 he would average $170 x 3.5 or about $595 per hour." Although this is theoretically possible, it is highly unlikely that anyone could achieve such glowing results playing the Five-count system these days.

Although definitely a winning strategy, the Five-count has many weaknesses. First of all, it loses effectiveness in shoe games, since the removal of such a small number of cards (i.e., only the 5s) influences the remaining deck composition much less, as explained in Myth #1, chapter 4. Second, the player must range his bets too drastically in order to take full advantage of situations when no 5s are left. This is always a dangerous practice, drawing immediate scrutiny from casino personnel. Third, other players at the table can too easily (albeit unwittingly) absorb the benefits of positive circumstances for themselves. Finally, the Five-count system provides no information about either the second most influential card for the player or the most abundant card in the deck, i.e., the Ace and the T respectively.

## Thorp's Ten-count Strategy

Card for card, it was a fact that the 5s being removed from a deck had the most effect upon the player's advantage. Conversely, Thorp also discovered that adding four T's to a deck increased the chances of winning the next hand by 1.89%. He proceeded to prove that the "richer" the deck was in 10-value cards, the greater the player's advantage became. Since in every deck there are four times as many T's than there are any other-valued card, this meant that there could be a much greater deviation from the norm when T's were tracked instead of 5s. Such variations meant even bigger possible gains for the player. Therefore, Thorp devised a much more powerful counting system, which came to be known as "Thorp's Ten-count."

Basically, the Ten-count system takes note of only two types of cards, the non-T's and the T's. By constantly comparing this ratio to the normal beginning ratio of 36 to 16, a competent counter is able to determine the degree of "10-richness" of the remaining deck at any given time. Dividing 36 by 16 gives 2.25, which represents the neutral condition of any deck. Thorp calculated that if this ratio dropped to 1.0 (i.e., an equal number of T's and non-T's remaining to be dealt), the player's advantage is approximately 9%. By ranging bets according to the 10-richness of the deck therefore, one could unquestionably make huge profits.

Thorp's Ten-count is more powerful than the Five-count, and it has the additional feature of informing the player exactly when to take insurance (i.e., whenever the ratio drops below 2.0). It unfortunately has significant disadvantages as well. One shortcoming is that, like the Five-count, it fails to recognize the tremendous importance of the Aces. This defect forces the conscientious counter to keep track of them separately, along with the number of T's and the number of non-T's seen. This practice necessarily involves keeping three separate numbers in mind throughout the game, updating them through not-so-simple arithmetic calculations as every card is dealt. Not an easy proposition for anyone, and simply too difficult for most people to attempt under actual casino conditions.

The main problem with the Ten-count, however, aside from its incessant and complicated mathematical calculations, is its difficult-to-memorize implementation tables. Only those players who have considerable math abilities, including excellent short-term memory skills, should even consider learning this system. For instance, in a single-deck game, after seeing four T's and eleven non-T's, you must realize that twenty-five non-T's and twelve T's remain available (subtracting 11 and 4 from 36 and 16 respectively), then do the necessary division in your head to arrive at the new rounded-off ratio figure of 2.08. Relating this number to Thorp's table, which you must have previously memorized, you quickly determine and place your correct-sized wager in time to play the next round. Then you must compare this figure to the most daunting of modification tables. Only then can you decide how best to actually play your hand.

Although Thorp's Ten-count system could still be a big moneymaker in the few single-deck games today, its necessary mathematical calculations are simply beyond most players' capabilities, especially under actual playing conditions. The speed of the game exerts too great a pressure on one's arithmetic skills and memory to make the Ten-count viable, and it is virtually impossible to use in shoe games. It is, nevertheless, worthwhile to obtain a copy of *Beat the Dealer* and study Thorp's systems and research tables. Interesting, truly exhaustive, and thoroughly reliable, they are essential reading for the serious student of the game. Every modern blackjack player owes Thorp a huge debt of gratitude and should rightly pay homage to his tremendous insight and ability. To call oneself a "counter" without being totally familiar with the original contributions of "the master" is but little short of blackjack blasphemy.

## Thorp's Point-count System

In his second edition of *Beat the Dealer,* Thorp presented a "point-count" system, which formed the basis of all subsequent counting systems and it provided the model for innumerable variations that have since evolved. Although Harvey Dubner's quite similar system appeared slightly before this publication, it primarily entailed modifications or simplifications of Thorp's original presentations and research.

Thorp was the first to note the relative values of each and every card (not just the 5s) to the player, as shown on the chart page 80 in chapter 4. With the help of Braun's more sophisticated computer programs, he determined that the player's advantage was greatest when more small-ranking or "low" cards (i.e., 2s, 3s, 4s, 5s, and 6s) were used up during play, leaving a surplus of 10-value cards (and Aces), the "high" cards, remaining to be dealt. It followed logically that the dealer had the odds with her after more high cards came out during the game.

This should begin to make sense for the reader as well: Players will win more money when there is a higher-than-normal concentration of T's and Aces available to appear. To be absolutely clear on this point, consider the hypothetical extreme, where *only* T's and Aces are left in the shoe. If such an opportunity presented itself, would you want to play under these circumstances? Stop and consider the situation for a minute, since it ably demonstrates the tremendous value to the player of Ace- and T-rich decks.

To determine what theoretical advantage would exist in such a scenario, examine each of the six possible hands that you could receive from a pool of only Aces and T's:

1. T,T versus A is a no-lose hand for you. Taking insurance, you only win even money if the dealer has a blackjack, but you win big if the dealer doesn't, since you would split the T's to the limit and necessarily win all of the splits. (In a shoe game there is the remote possibility that the dealer could end up with 11 Aces in a row and then draw a T to win with 21, but the odds of that happening are very low.)

2. When you have blackjack versus the dealer's Ace, by taking even money you would always get a sure win. If you decided to hold out for your 3-to-2 payoff, the worst that could happen would be a push.

3. Take advantage of the insurance proposition with A,A versus A and you will generally at least break even. If the dealer has the blackjack, you lose nothing. For those times that the dealer does not have a blackjack, splitting your Aces wins back more than the lost insurance, i.e., half of your original wager, since only rarely will two more Aces appear on both of your splits. The dealer is almost certain to bust, since the only way she could end up with a pat hand would be by drawing six more straight Aces—obviously an impossibility in a single-deck game, and highly unlikely in a shoe with the normal ratio of T's and Aces remaining to be dealt.

4. T,T versus the dealer's T represents several potential 21 wins for you when they are split to the max, if the dealer doesn't flip over an Ace. Pushing with 20s is the worst thing that can happen otherwise. When the dealer does get a blackjack, you lose only your one original wager, so on the whole this situation would make you money.

5. Your blackjack versus T wins you the 3-to-2 profits more often than not. When the dealer also has the natural, the resulting push doesn't cost you anything.

6. A,A versus T is your worst possible hand within this hypothetical situation. Splitting would usually provide very good moneymaking potential, since the dealer will not have an Ace in the hole more than 20% of the time. Your probable 21s will beat her 20 in most cases, but drawing an Ace on at least one of your splits is always a possibility, in which case you would only break even on the hand overall. As a whole, you would end up winning many more of these hands than you would lose, since the only way you could lose, other than the dealer's having a blackjack, is if you happen to draw two more Aces on your split.

Hopefully, you can see the huge advantage over the casino that you would enjoy if the only cards left in the game were Aces and T's. The wisdom of betting more in such a situation should be obvious. The extreme importance of the availability of 10-valued cards and Aces to the player should be growing much clearer.

Although it is not as evident as in the above ideal playing situation, the player also enjoys favorable odds when only slightly more T's and Aces as opposed to 2s through 6s are left in the shoe. Understanding why this condition represents bigger potential gains for the player is essential, no matter which counting system you may eventually choose to use. Similarly, when there are more low cards available to appear next, the knowledgeable card-caser enjoys an advantage over the non-counters as well, because he will then bet less and play more conservatively if he decides to play at all with such a poor count.

Consider the following reasons why knowing that there is either an excess of high cards or an excess of low cards available could help the player make better playing decisions:

1. More blackjacks than normal will occur when the shoe is Ace-T rich. The subsequent 3-to-2 payoff is a big plus for the player.

2. After doubling, which the player will do more frequently if the composition of the remaining cards favors T's and Aces, the player's final totals will tend to be higher, resulting in more wins.

3. When more T's than usual are available, the dealer will break

more frequently (being forced to hit her stiffs, and therefore ending up over 21 even more often). This provides the player with more than his usual winnings. (Unlike the dealer, the player has the option to stand on stiff hands in this situation, which represents a definite strategy gain.)

4. Knowing that a surplus of high cards exists is a powerful tool when determining the correct play. A player can alter BS accordingly, sometimes avoiding going over 21 by standing even when BS says to hit (e.g., 16 versus T, or 12 versus 3). (Chapter 7 provides all the necessary MBS information that should be applied by counters.)

5. With an abundance of T's and Aces in the deck, splitting will generate more doubling situations, which could prove favorable, and better totals for the player when doubling is not advisable.

6. With a significantly higher than normal density of T's available, the knowledgeable player is able to take full advantage of the profitable insurance wagers.

7. The surrender option offers the player an even bigger advantage when large quantities of T's are imminent.

8. When a surplus of low cards remains, the counter knows not to double weak beginning totals, especially certain soft hands against the dealers stiff up-cards, since the dealer is more apt to draw a pat hand. Against the player's potentially even weaker doubled-down total, this would be all the more disastrous.

9. Knowing enough to bet only the minimum (or not to play at all) when a superabundance of little cards are left in the shoe will save the player many otherwise wasted chips.

10. Knowing that a surplus of low cards exists is also a big advantage when deciding whether to hit or stand on certain totals. A player can more readily take a card on weak stiff hands without undue risk, even against the dealer's stiff up-cards. More often than not the hit (too dangerous to try normally according to BS) will result in pat hands.

Thorp's original point-count system still remains relevant, attractive, and practical even today because of its innovative methodology. Its combined simplicity and playing efficiency are impossible to beat. Basically, the system involves counting each card as it is seen: the low cards (2s, 3s, 4s, 5s, and 6s) as +1 each, and the high cards (10-value cards and Aces) as −1 each. The 7s, 8s, and 9s are nearly neutral to the player anyway, so they are ignored. Thus, keeping track of the various cards as they are used up normally in a game, the counting player can easily tell whether the remaining pool of cards contains an excess of high or low cards or if it is completely neutral.

For example, suppose that you saw the following ten cards appear during the first round of play immediately after a shuffle in a single-deck game, and you wanted to determine whether the remaining cards favored the player or the dealer:

2, 5, 7, A, 3, 9, T, 4, 6, 3

As you saw the 2 you would think to yourself, "+1." When the 5 appeared, you would mentally add another +1 and think, "The total is now +2." The 7 is neutral, so, ignoring it, you skip on to the A and think "−1," which brings the count total back down to +1 again. Similarly, the 3 takes the count up another point, the 9 is neutral, and the T pulls the count back down one point. You now have the count back at +1 once more. Adding in the 4, 6, and 3, the count climbs to +4 after this whole sequence of cards has been seen. This means that the odds of the player winning the next hand would be greater, since there are four more high cards (Aces and T's) than low ones (2s through 6s) now available to be dealt.

By keeping in mind just one number at a time in this manner, you will always know whether you or the dealer has the upper hand. Any positive point-count means that the odds favor you, while any negative point-count reflects an advantage for the house.

Generally speaking, it is advisable to play more aggressively when the count is positive and more conservatively when it is negative. In other words, when there are more high cards waiting to be dealt, you should stand, double, and split a bit more often than you would when abiding by normal BS. Conversely, when more low cards are ready to appear, you would tend to double and split less often but hit more frequently.

### Dubner's Hi-Low

Harvey Dubner introduced his version of this "Hi-Low" counting system in 1963. Although based upon Thorp's and Braun's research, its beauty lay primarily in its added simplicity. Much easier to implement than Thorp's Ten-count system, Dubner's Hi-Low was almost as powerful, and it subsequently brought viable card-counting within the grasp of the average blackjack player. Dubner suggested the same basic card values (i.e., low cards were counted as +1 and high cards as −1, while 7s, 8s, and 9s continued to be ignored). Braun improved upon Dubner's ideas by developing correct wagering and playing strategies for this counting system, which remain state-of-the-art today. Known interchangeably now as "Thorp's Point-count," "Dubner's Hi-Low," and "Braun's Plus-Minus," these three systems are virtually identical. It is still the most highly recommended and successful of all counting regimes ever devised, whatever label one chooses to attach to it. Since Dubner was the first to describe and propound the virtues of this counting system it is only fair that we refer to it as he did and call it the "Hi-Low."

## Hi-Low Wagering Methods

*Plus-count Wagering* Using the Hi-Low system, players were quick to realize that they had an advantage over the casino whenever the count was at all positive. Even novice counters immediately adopted a winning strategy known as "plus-count wagering" in which they increased their bets a little whenever the count indicated a surplus of T's and Aces remaining to be dealt. They would then proceed to play their hands according to BS.

Plus-count wagering goes like this: Beginning fresh with each round of play, the cards are counted as −1 for Aces and T's, and +1 for each 2 through 6 as seen. If the round ends with a positive result, a two-unit bet is placed for the next hand. If that round produces a plus-count as well, the two-unit bet is increased to three units, and so on. Whenever a round ends neutral or negative in total, the size of the bet is maintained or reduced respectively. Each round is considered a completely separate and distinct entity, and subsequent wagers are made according to the plus or minus results of the most recent round of play only. There is no attempt to remember the count throughout the whole deck or shoe, nor to modify BS plays because of it.

This simple plus-count wagering strategy remains a mildly effective system, especially for players who find themselves sitting at full tables, and particularly if they are not yet entirely competent counters. With no numbers to keep in mind, it takes minimal effort to glance around the table after each deal is over in order to size one's bet for the next hand. It is an ideal winning system for those who are not really concerned about making much money from the game but would rather enjoy the free drinks and perhaps socialize while they play. Plus-count wagering demands no concentration or playing skill of any sort beyond knowing the correct BS and applying it. Although this system will seldom make you much money, about nine sessions out of ten it will keep you from losing your stake.

The main drawback with the plus-count betting strategy is that players are sometimes wagering quite inappropriately. Suppose the first round after a shuffle results in a particularly bad figure, say $-6$, and the second one produces a good count of $+4$. Playing according to plus-count wagering, the player would increase his bet after the second round even though the overall count is still negative. This player has bumped up his bet when he is actually at a disadvantage. Although certainly better than just wagering blindly with no count strategy at all, the plus-count leaves much to be desired and can not be recommended generally.

*Running-count Wagering* The Hi-Low number you keep updating round after round as the cards fall has come to be known as the "running count" (RC). Although the RC always tells you whom the odds favor before any particular hand, it does not always indicate to what degree or how much the advantage is. Many beginning counters make money consistently (playing in single-deck games primarily) by merely ranging their bets in direct proportion to the RC whenever it is positive. This method, known as running-count wagering, is used successfully in conjunction with BS alone. It is an easy yet very effective counting system to implement. For the casual blackjack player it may be a completely satisfactory winning strategy in itself.

## The Hi-Low RC Bet-Ranging Guide

Note: In using this guide, begin counting at − 3.

| If RC Is | Bet This Many Units |
|---|---|
| − 6 or less | (no bet—leave table) |
| − 5 to + 1 | 1 (the minimum bet) |
| + 2 | 2 |
| + 3 | 3 |
| + 4 | 4 |
| + 5 | 5 |
| + 6 | 6 |
| + 7 | 7 |
| + 8 | 8 |
| + 9 | 9 |
| + 10 or more | 10 (suggested upper limit) |

To use the RC wagering system most effectively, *start* your RC at − 3 after each shuffle. The actual RC after a shuffle is zero, of course, but for the purposes of this bet-ranging guide, always begin counting at − 3 in order to give yourself some built-in protection. This margin of safety will keep you from excessive overbetting if the RC happens to soar early in the shoe. If the RC falls to − 6 or less, stop playing and wait for a new shuffle or at least until the count comes back up. As long as the RC remains below + 2, bet the minimum, i.e., one unit. Increase your bet by one unit (or less if possible, perhaps by $1 if the minimum bet is $5) for every whole number that the RC climbs above 2. Under no circumstances, however, should you range your bets up to more than ten units, or 2% of your total bankroll. Under this easy-to-remember system the size of your bets is governed by the RC itself. A beginning counter can usually recover the count whenever he happens to lose track of it, simply by looking at the amount that was bet on the last hand.

*True-count Wagering* For shoe games, which are by far the most common these days, ranging one's bet simply according to the RC alone is not reliable enough for serious counters. In a counting example earlier in this chapter, a RC of + 4 represented a significant advantage for the player, since it existed in a single-deck game. The same RC of +4, however, would indicate a far less favorable situation if it occurred at the beginning of a six-deck shoe game. While it is true that there would still be four more high cards than low ones available to be dealt, with six times the number of cards in the pool the odds of drawing one of those "extra" high cards is considerably less.

Therefore, to obtain an accurate indication of the advantage, it is necessary to divide the RC by the number of remaining decks yet to be seen. This figure is obviously much more reliable and is known simply as the true count (TC), since it indicates the RC per deck. Although not quite as accurate as Thorp's complete point-count system, this estimated TC is virtually just as reliable to use in determining the proper size of your next bet and in modifying BS when applicable.

In the single-deck example mentioned above, the RC of +4 represents a TC of approximately +5 (+4 ÷ ⁴/₅, the remaining number of whole decks still available to be dealt). At the beginning of a six-deck shoe, however, the same +4 RC produces a TC of less than 1 (+4 divided by almost 6—the number of decks remaining in the shoe). While you would still have some advantage playing BS in a shoe game under these circumstances, it would not be enough to justify increasing your next wager beyond the minimum allowable bet. The rounded-off TC would be only +1.

After a little practice at converting RC's into TC's, you will note that in all shoe games (where the plastic shuffle card is normally placed more than one full deck from the last card), the TC's will necessarily be less than positive RC's, because you must always divide by more than one unseen deck. In single-deck games, TC's will always be greater than positive RC's, since you will be dividing by less than one (full deck). Of course, when the RC is negative, just the opposite occurs. In a six-deck shoe, for example, the TC's are never as good as positive RC's, but never as bad as negative RC's. Use the Hi-Low TC practice exercises at the end of this chapter to become totally familiar with converting RC's into TC's.

The biggest advantage of knowing the TC lies in its ability to properly indicate the size of one's next wager, no matter how many decks are being used in the game. This system is, not surprisingly, described as true-count wagering. A counter who combines appropriate true-count bet ranges with correct MBS plays as explained in chapter 7 is doing everything possible to maximize his advantage. Yes, professional counting is as simple as that.

Proper TC wagering is likely the least understood calculation, and consequently the most misplayed aspect of the game, for otherwise competent counters. Rarely is this vital aspect of play even mentioned in blackjack literature. Take the time now to commit this essential piece of knowledge to memory, and you will never again need to worry whether your bets are sized properly. Correct TC wagering is calculated as follows:

From the Kelly Criterion discussed in chapter 4, it is clear that betting in direct proportion to your advantage provides the most reliable long-term profits. Your exact percentage advantage, however, is not always easily determined. It depends mostly upon the TC, but the liberality of the rules being used should also be considered. Naturally, the advantage provided by any given TC will vary directly with the playing conditions in place at the time. Therefore, if you find yourself playing under restrictive rules, you should range your bets slightly more conservatively than the conservative TC Bet-Ranging Chart below indicates; when the rules are exceptionally good, slightly higher.

---

*A player's advantage is calculated by adding .515 to the profit expectation derived from BS playing conditions, then multiplying this figure by the TC.*

---

In other words, playing where your BS profit expectation is zero (i.e., no advantage for the casino or yourself because of the rules), your advantage in percent is generally half the TC at any given time. You should never, therefore, bet more than this percentage of your total blackjack-playing bankroll on any one hand—ever, under any circumstances. Betting more than your percentage advantage is courting financial disaster.

For example, if your entire blackjack bankroll amounted to only $500 and the TC climbed to +6, then your next bet should ideally be $15 (i.e., 6% x ½ x 500, or 3% of $500). But from chapter 5 it is clear that, in order to maximize gains while minimizing risks, you should never wager more than 2% of your total bankroll on any single hand no matter how good the situation appears. Whenever you exceed 2% you are in a sense overbetting, even though the TC may justify a higher wager because of your percentage advantage. Because 2% of $500 is only $10, your bankroll is too small to allow you to take full advantage of TC's over +4. No matter what size your bankroll is, this limit comes into play. To be absolutely safe, your wagers should range smoothly from a maximum bet of 2% of your bankroll down to nothing, while staying in accordance with your actual playing advantage determined by the TC.

This is one reason it is advisable to play at tables that offer the lowest limits. There you can bet the table minimum when the TC is 0 or less and range your wagers upward to eight units or more, as the TC wagering charts below dictate, without violating your 2% guideline.

## Conservative TC Bet-Ranging Chart

| If TC Is | Bet This Many Units |
|---|---|
| −5 or less | (no bet—leave table) |
| −4 to +1 | 1 (minimum bet) |
| +2 to +4 | 2 |
| +5 or +6 | 3 |
| +7 or +8 | 4 |
| +9 or +10 | 5 |
| +11 or +12 | 6 |
| +13 or +14 | 7 |
| +15 or more | 8 (upper limit) |

Note: The number of units bet is approximately *half* the TC in the above example.

## Aggressive TC Bet-Ranging Chart

| If TC Is | Bet This Many Units |
|---|---|
| − or 0 | 1 (minimum bet) |
| +1 | 2 |
| +2 | 3 |
| +3 | 4 |
| +4 | 5 |
| +5 | 6 |
| +6 | 7 |
| +7 or more | 8 (upper limit) |

Note: The number of units bet is approximately *equal* to the TC in the chart.

Both of these charts are meant only as rough guidelines, not dyed-in-the-wool dictums to be followed rigidly, especially when the heat is on. Keep them in mind, but also remember that a gradual change in the size of your wager is far less apt to draw attention or arouse suspicion. Depending upon the size of your bankroll, you can figure roughly what the dollar figure for each bet will be. With a little panache, you may be able to pull off a single jump from one to ten units successfully, but it is certainly not recommended.

Just as credit card companies benefit from monthly interest payments when their clients spend beyond their means, so casinos try to coerce their blackjack patrons into overbetting. When table minimums are raised to $25, any player whose bankroll is less than $1,250 can't play at all without dancing with gambler's ruin. This is exactly what casino management hopes to encourage. Novice players and experienced counters alike continually fall into this subtle trap.

Avoid overbetting by figuring out in advance exactly what your maximum bet can be when you comply with the 2% Rule. Then find a table whose minimum bet allows a range of ten betting units *within your betting limit* and decide how you will increase your wagers as the TC climbs.

For example, if your total blackjack bankroll is $1,000, your maximum bet will be $20. Under absolutely no conditions will you wager more than $20 on a single hand. At a $2 table your bet-ranging could look like the following hypothetical sample:

## Sample Conservative TC Wagering Guide: $2 Table

| If TC Is | | Bet |
|---|---|---|
| − or 0 | | (no play) |
| +1 | | $2 |
| +2 | | $4 |
| +3 | | $6 |
| +4 | | $8 |
| +5 | | $10 |
| +6 | | $12 |
| +7 | | $14 |
| +8 | | $16 |
| +9 | | $18 |
| +10 or more | | $20 |

## Sample Aggressive TC Wagering Guide: $2 Table

| If TC Is | | Bet |
|---|---|---|
| − or 0 | | $2 |
| +1 | | $5 |
| +2 | | $10 |
| +3 | | $15 |
| +4 or more | | $20 |

Under the same circumstances, at a $5 minimum table your bet-ranging might look something like this:

## Sample Conservative TC Wagering Guide: $5 Table

| If TC Is | | Bet |
|---|---|---|
| − or 0 | | (no play) |
| +1 | | $5 |
| +2 | | $6 |
| +3 | | $7 |
| +4 | | $9 |
| +5 | | $11 |
| +6 | | $13 |
| +7 | | $15 |
| +8 | | $17 |
| +9 | | $19 |
| +10 or more | | $20 |

## Sample Aggressive TC Wagering Guide: $5 Table

| If TC Is | | Bet |
|---|---|---|
| − or 0 | | (no play) |
| +1 | | $5 |
| +2 | | $10 |
| +3 | | $15 |
| +4 or more | | $20 |

Similarly, with a bankroll of only a grand, your wagers could safely range from $5 to $20 something like this:

| If TC Is | | Bet |
|---|---|---|
| below 2 | _____ | (no bet—leave table) |
| −2 to +1 | _____ | $5 |
| +2 or +3 | _____ | $8 |
| +4 or +5 | _____ | $11 |
| +6 or +7 | _____ | $14 |
| +8 or +9 | _____ | $17 |
| +10 or more | _____ | $20 |

Under the following bet-ranging system, you could have a total blackjack bankroll of as little as $500 and still not violate the 2% rule. You would not be fully exploiting your TC advantages, but at least you would not be risking gambler's ruin.

| If TC Is | | Bet |
|---|---|---|
| below 2 | _____ | (no bet—leave table) |
| −2 to +1 | _____ | $5 |
| +2 or +3 | _____ | $6 |
| +4 or +5 | _____ | $7 |
| +6 or +7 | _____ | $8 |
| +8 or +9 | _____ | $9 |
| +10 or more | _____ | $10 |

It should be pointed out here that if your entire bankroll is only $500 or less, and the table minimum is $10, then you are certain to be overbetting on almost every hand. Sit down and play under such conditions only if you are willing to risk losing your playing stakes several times in a row, or perhaps going completely broke because of long runs of weak hands. In such a situation, Wonging is strongly recommended (see chapter 5). Playing BS and counting cards only guarantees winning over the long haul; in the short run anything can happen and will, but if you expect the worst you can never be disappointed.

The main thing to remember when planning your TC wagering leeway is not to exceed the 2% limit on any bet. It's not critical to range your bets perfectly within this limit, as long as they always vary directly with the TC. This way you are sure to be betting more when the counts are good and less when they drop, all the while staying within your betting limit.

## Other Counting Systems

During the thirty-odd years since the first viable counting system was introduced, dozens of "new and improved" counting systems have been offered for sale to unsuspecting blackjack players eager for easy winnings. Each additional system sported a slightly different variation of the original Hi-Low model. Each promised more simplicity, accuracy, or playing efficiency than the one before. Averaging $200 to $300 apiece, they all incorporated nearly the same basic counting practices that Thorp, Dubner, and Braun introduced. In researching the material for this book, several of these highly touted "miracle" systems were purchased for review. Not surprisingly, none turned out to be better than the original Hi-Low.

One early "advanced" system offered for sale at $1,000 merely assigned different card point-values to be counted as follows: Aces $= -10$ each; 9s and 10s $= -5$ each; 5s $= +10$ each; 2s, 3s, 4s, 6s, and 7s $= +5$ each; 8s alone were ignored as neutral. This was obviously a cumbersome system to employ for an entirely negligible advantage over the tried and true Hi-Low. The values following would serve the same purpose and be much simpler to tally: Aces $= -2$ each; 9s and 10s $= -1$ each; 5s $= +2$ each; and 2s, 3s, 4s, 6s, and 7s $= +1$ each; 8s ignored. Even this simplification would not be worth the extra mental effort involved. Be happy if you were not one of the poor unfortunates who shelled out big bucks for this system.

### Revere's Advanced Point Count

Lawrence Revere offered an "Advanced Point Count" system for sale in the early 1970s which became quite popular. It assigned new values to the cards as seen during the game: Aces $= -4$; T's $= -3$; 9s $= -1$;

8s = 0; 7s and 2s = 2; 6s, 4s and 3s = 3; and 5s = 4. Revere's system was powerful, and still is, but only truly dedicated and mathematically adept players ever master it well enough to actually implement successfully under casino conditions.

## Cardoza/Silberstang Variation

In 1982, Edwin Silberstang and Avery Cardoza claimed to have systems that were definite improvements over Hi-Low primarily because their TC's were more accurate. Instead of dividing the RC by the number of decks unseen, they suggested dividing it by the number of half-decks unseen to obtain a truer TC.

The problems with the Silberstang/Cardoza approach are many. First, whether the remaining unseen cards are rounded off to whole decks or half-decks, the resulting TC is still just an estimate, so the extra mental step involved is difficult to justify for such a questionable gain. Second, a TC based upon whole decks is a simpler concept to grasp and negates the need to memorize new MBS tables (which necessarily list indices half the magnitude of standard Hi-Low tables). Third, discriminating players take note of half-deck variations as a matter of course within their normal TC calculations anyway, without necessarily converting the remaining cards into half-deck groups. For example, if the RC is +7, and one's estimate suggests that there is closer to three and a half decks left rather than an even three or four, it is no more difficult to divide by the mixed number and come up with +2 than it is to divide by 7, which equals +1. (Remember that TC's in this proposed system are represented as only half of normal TC's, so it works out exactly the same.) Any advantage to the player from using such a slightly more accurate TC is virtually imperceptible. An additional problem with this system is that the Aces are completely ignored as neutral cards, which creates even more troubles. Luckily, the Cardoza system only costs $129 plus shipping and handling for anyone who might still be interested.

## Einstein Variation

Charles Einstein, in 1968, was the first to suggest that Aces should be removed from the RC altogether. Because of their dual nature—i.e., the fact that they can be regarded as high or low cards depending upon the situation—Einstein claimed that Aces should be counted as neutral. It is a somewhat valid point theoretically, but ignoring the Aces in the RC is obviously problematic. Several other authors (e.g. Griffen, Cardoza, Revere, Silberstang, Humble and Cooper) promoting their own "unique" counting systems later also jumped aboard the Aces = 0 bandwagon. Although some of their systems were reasonably good and are still being used successfully by assorted players, they all possessed at least two very serious inherent drawbacks.

First, in blackjack, Aces are the most important card in the deck. The number of Aces available to be dealt is extremely important to the player; therefore, if Aces are not included in the RC, they must be kept track of separately by means of what is known as an Ace "side-count." The maintenance of any side-count is difficult to master for even professional counters, since it represents an additional set of numbers that must be kept in mind throughout the shoe. Unless you have an exceptional aptitude for this type of mental gymnastics, side-counts are neither feasible nor advisable.

Second, if the Aces are counted as 0 in the RC, the "balance" of the complete-deck point-values is necessarily disturbed. An otherwise neutral deck would appear to be +4, because of the surplus of little cards being counted as "pluses" if the Aces were ignored. The point-values of the cards had to be adjusted to restore point-count equilibrium to the shoes. Consequently the lowly 2 was sacrificed, being demoted from +1 to be considered as 0, along with the Aces, 7s, 8s, and 9s.

Ignoring the 2s only exacerbates the problem. It is an unacceptable practice, since it forces an additional fault upon the counting system by calling this obvious plus-card a neutral merely in order to justify the questionable practice of counting the Aces as 0. A more reasonable plus-count adjustment was suggested by Revere in his "Advanced Plus-Minus" system, in which he counted the 9s (which are rated slightly negative anyway) as −1 to compensate for Aces equaling 0.

While it is true that Aces normally act as the highest cards (boasting a value of 11), they do occasionally masquerade as low cards (meekly offering up a value of just 1) if necessary. According to Stanford Wong's research, however, counting the Aces as −1 rather than 0 in the RC can more accurately determine proper bet-ranging. This is more vital than playing absolutely correct MBS (and insurance situations) because of more specific Ace information obtained through side-counts. It is far more important to have correct amounts wagered, i.e., always in direct proportion to one's advantage, since these situations occur much more frequently than the rare MBS adjustments or insurance opportunities.

In other words, slightly less accurate plays when these rarer circumstances arise will hurt you less than regularly having the wrong-sized bet out. Since Aces are generally played as high cards and are a benefit to the player when available to be dealt, it is unreasonable to discount their overall impact on the TC simply because they sometimes act as low cards. Therefore, any advantage that might possibly be gained by changing the cards' point-values in the RC merely to account for this duality of the Aces is certainly more than offset by the additional effort required to track them separately by means of side-counting.

### Thorp's Ultimate

Thorp eventually came up with a system that provided almost perfect wagering information. He called his last program the "Thorp Ultimate," and it represented a 99.6% correct betting strategy. The point-values were assigned as follows: 2s $= 5$, 3s $= 6$, 4s $= 8$, 5s $= 11$, 6s $= 6$, 7s $= 4$, 8s $= 0$, 9s $= -3$, T's $= -7$, and Aces $= -9$. Unfortunately, the Thorp Ultimate is so difficult to count and implement, it is not worth serious consideration at all. Imagine using this system, trying to tally up the RC at a full table after the dealer flips over a blackjack and begins scooping up the cards! For anyone other than mathematical magicians, it is totally impractical for actual casino use.

At the other extreme, J. L. Patterson's *Blackjack: A Winner's Handbook* (1990 edition) suggests that no counting system is dependable these days since "card counting doesn't always work." Patterson cites examples of players who sometimes win when the count is actually negative and of players losing while the count is very positive. He claims that counting works best when the game is played on computers, but not very well in real casinos. Apparently Patterson cannot accept the inherent short-term fluctuations that inevitably occur within probability theory and has thrown the proverbial blackjack "baby" out with its bathwater. (Gullible readers can purchase Patterson's "TARGET 21 Home-Study Course," which is basically an empirical approach to the game, for a mere $295—plus shipping and handling, of course.)

## Choosing a System That Is Right for You

Selecting which counting system you will learn and use is a very personal decision. Each player must be comfortable with his choice, not merely accepting recommendations made by various pitchmen trying to peddle their wares. The reader is encouraged to explore systems other than the Hi-Low and to reach independent conclusions. After all, the study of blackjack is a completely open-ended pursuit, and no single counting system holds all of the cards (excuse the pun). Most players continue to search for ever-increasing advantages over the casinos. The selection of the right system for you, however, is far too important a decision to be left to chance. Here are four factors worth considering:

1. Exactly how serious are you about winning? How much time, money, and energy are you willing to expend learning to implement the specific counting system of your choice?
2. Is the system graduated to allow sequential stages of successful playing as you learn it?
3. Is the system authentic and reliable? Is it backed by reputable research? Has it proven itself over the years? Or is it some fly-by-night fast-buck artist's scheme?
4. Is the system practical for your use under actual casino conditions? There's no point trying to master one that is too complex or that provides only mediocre results.

There is a point for most players where the law of diminishing returns sets in. This occurs when it simply isn't worth learning a slightly more efficient system either because of its cost or because it may be extremely tedious and cumbersome to use. Some are so mentally exhausting that they drain the enjoyment from the game, and all for negligible gain.

This chapter provides the necessary information for you to choose one of the simplest and best systems currently available. The Hi-Low system outlined earlier is sanctioned by five of the most respected names in blackjack research: Thorp, Braun, Dubner, Revere, and Wong. Although simple to learn and implement, Hi-Low is one of the most efficient counting systems ever devised when used with its appropriate MBS. I highly recommended that you master the Hi-Low system first, even if you decide to adopt a possibly more powerful counting strategy at some later date. The Hi-Low meets or exceeds all of the relevant criteria regarding the selection of a counting system.

Some systems are so very complex that they are impractical for actual casino use. Only those players who aspire to be truly dedicated professionals should even consider the most comprehensive and efficient systems—whatever they may be. Remember that the "absolute best" system, if such a thing exists short of incorporating the use of a computer right at the table, will necessarily be extremely difficult to master and use. Furthermore, it will be only very slightly better than several very good systems (like Hi-Low) that are relatively easy to employ. What most people fail to realize is that their overall playing advantage differs by less than 1 percent between any good system and the most efficient ones. The differences in total dollars earned for the players are negligible.

An old English expression, "Penny wise, but pound foolish," springs to mind here. Is it worth it to you to learn plays that you will be required to make less than once every thousand or more hands? Probably not. The final consideration that you must come to grips with is this: Dozens of extra study hours, or more realistically study weeks, are required to master any of the more complex counting systems. You must decide if the additional effort involved justifies the extremely slight monetary advantages that they may provide for you. Spending hundreds of dollars to purchase a more complicated counting program (that you may not be able to actually use anyway) in order to win a few extra cents over the years, seems a questionable plan at best.

You have all of the essential elements of the Hi-Low counting system in your hands at this moment. By all means, investigate other systems if you wish to satisfy your curiosity, but learn this one first—just in case you never get around to examining another. The Hi-Low has more power than anyone could ever hope to use in a lifetime, and I recommend it as the best overall blackjack card-counting system in existence.

## Hi-Low Counting Practice Exercise 1
### The Running Count

Each question represents the various hands obtained at the table, by yourself, by other players, and by the dealer. Some are busts, as in real life. Carry over the RC from one question to the next, just as you would in the normal round-to-round play of any game. For optimal learning, cover the RC answer column until after you have finished counting each round; then you can immediately confirm the correct RC.

| Exposed Cards | | | | | RC |
|---|---|---|---|---|---|
| 1. A,2,3 | T,4,8 | 5,T,A,7 | 6,7,9 | T,2,2,A,A | 0 |
| 2. 4,9,7 | 5,8,A,T | A,T | 3,3,7,2,9 | 8,3,T | 1 |
| 3. 6,6,6 | 2,3,9,A,T | 8,7,2,9 | 3,3,4,A,7 | | 7 |
| 4. A,5,A,3,4,2,8 | A,A,5,T | 9,9 | 8,A | 4,9,T | 6 |
| 5. 6,T,T | T,A | 9,2,T | T,5,T | 8,3,T | 2 |
| 6. 3,T,A,7 | T,4,T | A,3,4,8,T | 7,A,A,A,6,T | | −3 |
| 7. T,6,T | 5,T,A,9 | 8,A,T | 9,3,T | 4,T,2,T | −7 |
| 8. 4,3,7,2,A | 2,T,4,T | 3,3,7,2,9 | T,3,T | | −3 |
| 9. 8,2,7,T | 4,4,6,2,9 | T,3,2,A,5 | 5,5,5,A,8 | | 4 |
| 10. 5,4,2,T | T,3,2,A,3 | 2,9,3,4 | A,2,T | 2,9,T | 9 |

## Hi-Low Counting Practice Exercise 2
## The True Count

Carry over the RC from the end of one question to the next, just as you would in the round-after-round play of a shoe game. Then apply the new "Decks Unseen" number to determine the correct TC at the end of each question, always rounding off the TC to the nearest integer (round halves up).

The RC is always the only number you need to remember from one question (round) to the next, since the "Decks Unseen" arbitrarily changes for this exercise.

| Exposed Cards From the Shoe | Decks Unseen | TC | RC |
|---|---|---|---|
| 1. T,4,8  5,T,A,7  6,7,9  A,A,T,T | 5 | −1 | −4 |
| 2. A,T  5,A,A,T,9  T,3,2,T  T,6,2 | 2 | −1 | −3 |
| 3. 3,5,T  T,T  6,A,T  4,T,T  T,A | 4 | −2 | −8 |
| 4. 3,3,5,T  8,7,T  9,9  T,T | 5 | −2 | −9 |
| 5. A,2,3  T,4,8  5,T,A,7  6,7,9 | 3 | −3 | −8 |
| 6. 4,9,7  5,8,A,T  A,T  3,3,7,2,9 | 5 | −1 | −7 |
| 7. 3,3,4,A,7  6,6,6  2,3,9,A,T  8,7,2,9 | 2 | 0 | −1 |
| 8. T,6,T  5,T,A,9  8,A,T  9,3,T | 3 | −2 | −5 |
| 9. 4,3,7,2,A  2,T,4,T  3,3,7,2,9  T,3,T | 4 | 0 | −1 |
| 10. 8,2,7,9  4,4,6,2,9  7,3,2,A,5 | 4 | 2 | 6 |

If you want to place bets of appropriate size, it is absolutely essential that you learn to calculate accurate TC's quickly. With a little practice you can learn to do the arithmetic almost automatically. You will notice that positive TC's are always larger than RC's in single-deck games, because you are dividing by less than 1. In multiple-deck games where the shuffle card is placed more than a deck from the end of the shoe, TC's will always be less than RC's, since you will be dividing by numbers greater than 1. (Of course, just the opposite occurs with negative counts.) Remember to retain the plus or minus signs in your answers. To make sure you understand the concept and can do the proper calculations, try this short TC practice exercise:

## Hi-Low Counting Practice Exercise 3
### The True Count

To determine the TC at any point in any game, divide the RC by the number of unseen decks remaining to be dealt. Always round off TC's, rounding up exact halves to the nearest whole integer.

| RC | | Unseen Decks | | TC |
|---|---|---|---|---|
| 3 | _____ | 1 | _____ | 3 |
| −6 | _____ | 3 | _____ | −2 |
| 8 | _____ | 2 | _____ | 4 |
| −4 | _____ | 4 | _____ | −1 |
| 10 | _____ | 2 | _____ | 5 |
| −12 | _____ | 3 | _____ | −4 |
| −2 | _____ | 2 | _____ | −1 |
| −8 | _____ | 4 | _____ | −2 |
| 14 | _____ | 2 | _____ | 7 |
| 0 | _____ | 5 | _____ | 0 |
| −5 | _____ | 3 | _____ | −2 |
| 4 | _____ | 3 | _____ | 1 |
| 6 | _____ | 4 | _____ | 2 |
| 1 | _____ | 3 | _____ | 0 |
| −1 | _____ | 2 | _____ | 0 |
| 7 | _____ | 4 | _____ | 2 |
| 4 | _____ | 3 | _____ | 1 |
| 9 | _____ | 4 | _____ | 2 |
| −17 | _____ | 3 | _____ | −6 |
| −8 | _____ | 3 | _____ | −3 |

Remember that TC's are only approximations at best, since you always need to estimate the number of remaining decks. For more accurate TC's, you may want to use a more exact number for the unseen cards, by guessing them to the nearest half-deck or even quarter-deck. For example, in the last line of the exercise above, if you figured there were $3\frac{1}{4}$ decks remaining instead of 3; $8 \times \frac{4}{13} = \frac{32}{13}$, i.e., $2\frac{6}{13}$, which rounds off to −2 instead of −3. This degree of precision requires more math ability, and for most players the gain is not worth the mental strain involved.

# 7

# Modified Basic Strategy

If all blackjack players consistently played out their hands according to correct BS as presented in chapter 3, there is no doubt that the casinos would be forced to discontinue the game. Playing perfect BS under favorable blackjack rules cuts the casino percentage advantage to zero (or less, when liberal rules variations apply). Expenses would far exceed any profits they could hope to obtain. They would be able to offer their patrons only games such as roulette, craps, slots, etc., in which skill is not a factor. (Perhaps poker, too, could continue to exist, because the casinos automatically take their percentage from every pot won, no matter how skilled the players.) But it is certain that if everyone adopted perfect BS, the house couldn't possibly make enough money from blackjack to pay its employees' wages, let alone all the additional overhead costs involved. The game as we know it would quickly wither and die.

## Introduction to MBS

Most casino-goers have heard by now that blackjack is the only game that can be consistently beaten through skillful, intelligent play. This fact alone, no doubt, draws many to the game. Unfortunately, the majority of players barely have a cursory knowledge of the rules, let alone how to play 100% correctly using BS. Strangely enough, a recent survey showed that up to 95% of all players rely merely upon hunches and intuition for as much as 20% of their plays. This is the main factor that generates big profits for the casinos. After all, most players are at the blackjack tables primarily for fun rather than for profit. To them, the game is simply another form of recreation, to be equated with taking in a show or spending the afternoon at the beach. Few expect to actually win money, since they "know" intuitively that the casinos must have some advantage, or else they couldn't stay in business. Most players believe that in blackjack, as in the other casino games offered to them, if they are lucky they'll win; otherwise they'll lose. But, as the lyrics to an old song astutely point out, "It ain't necessarily so!"

Consider the fact that less than 10% of all blackjack players have ever read a book on the subject or have stumbled upon an accurate BS playing chart. Of the few who have, less than half proceed to take that additional baby-step of committing to memory and using this beneficial information. Of the thousands of players I have observed over the years, it is a generous estimate to say that even one in twenty was playing according to correct BS. With less than 5% of the blackjack-playing public knowing what they should do with any particular hand they might receive, it is no wonder that the casinos cherish this game above all others.

"A little knowledge is a dangerous thing!" This old adage is particularly applicable to blackjack players. It is quite common to encounter players who have aquired a smattering of reasonably good playing skills and therefore fully expect to end up winning money from the game. After all, they know the game can indeed be beaten simply through smart play. Unfortunately, these same people consistently make enough mistakes to keep the odds tilted well in the casinos' favor. The casinos openly welcome these players night after night, since they contribute to the house's coffers far more than they walk away with during their odd winning sessions.

These experienced and often grizzled gamblers may know enough to stand with their stiff totals when the dealer is showing stiff up-cards, to double on 10s and 11s, to always split Aces and 8s, and maybe even to never take insurance; but often, for example, their "soft" playing skills are weak or virtually nonexistent. They may not know, for example, to hit their hand of A,3,4 versus 9. They may not be sure of which Ace-combinations require doubling. Simply because they have enjoyed a few successful playing sessions in the past, they are confident that they now understand the game well enough to beat it over time. Unfortunately, this is simply not the case.

Regularly overbetting and then chasing their losses, these "dangerous" gamblers typically lack even a modicum of money management skills. While they are quick to give advice and chastise others for, say, splitting T's, they themselves are quite apt to stand with two 9s versus an 8 or routinely commit other such subtle BS sins. Sadly, their few persistent mistakes are more than enough to provide the house with a permanent and substantial edge, thus ensuring that these "knowledgeable" players never end up winners in the long run. The most pathetic thing about them, however, is that they are totally unaware of their own ignorance. They are continually disgusted with their bad "luck" and cannot understand why they lose their playing stakes so often, even though they know the game so well! Ignorance provides very little bliss in the game of blackjack.

While it is true that "premium" players (those at the $100 tables and higher) generally play slightly better than those at the lower-minimum tables, it is still extremely rare to find even one of these "high rollers" who really knows what he's doing or, more precisely, why he's doing it. It is sometimes amusing, while on a break, to watch the "whales" (big bettors who shove out a grand or more for each wager) continually misplaying hand after hand. They lose consistently, as the pit bosses look on and nod approvingly regarding their questionable plays. One such whale who comes to mind (possibly due to his enormous bulk—he could barely balance on the stool and would often stand behind the table because of this) lost two blue chips ($2,000) on one hand after hitting his 13 versus a 2. Since the count was quite positive at the time, I am certain that he was not playing a modified strategy of any kind. Most likely he had some vague recollection about hitting 12s versus 3s or 13s versus 2s, but couldn't quite remember which was the correct play—assuming that he cared enough to have so much as glanced at a BS chart somewhere previously. "A fool and his money are soon parted," as the saying goes; how these people got their money in the first place remains a mystery.

Before actually delving into MBS charts, which involve changing BS plays according to what the TC is, it should be emphasized here that there is more than one "correct" basic playing strategy, even for the noncounter. Readers should be aware that 100% accurate BS varies a little with the rules that happen to apply in any particular casino. The BS introduced in chapter 3 is the general playing strategy that should be followed in the vast majority of games being offered today. It represents less than 0.02% loss of advantage if used under any other playing conditions. However, for those students of the game who would like to know the very best plays to make under somewhat more unusual circumstances, the following information will be of some use.

## Single-Deck MBS

Proper single-deck basic strategy, for instance, is slightly different from proper shoe strategy, even when the rules are identical. You will probably never actually use this information, since single-deck games are offered so rarely; and when they are, their rules are so restrictive that you would be foolish to play them anyway. It is worth looking at the absolutely correct single-deck plays, though, if only for a better understanding of MBS theory. Here, then, are the modifications to BS that you should adopt for use under normal single-deck playing conditions:

1. 2s and 3s are not to be split versus the dealer's 2, nor 3s versus 3. Split 4s versus 4, 5, or 6 only if doubling-down after splitting is allowed.
2. Double A,2 and A,3 versus 4, 5, or 6; A,6 versus 2; A,8 versus 6; 8 versus 5 or 6; 9 versus 2; and 11 versus A.
3. A,7 stands versus A.

You should note that even these changes to BS cannot be applied accurately to all single-deck games. Computer studies have shown that certain plays should be made only under very specific circumstances: whether surrender is offered; whether doubling after splitting is allowed; whether any two cards may be doubled, or only 10s and 11s; whether the dealer stands on all 17s, and so on. Understand that every rule change theoretically demands its own picayune BS modification. For instance, you are sometimes required to double your 5,3 versus a 6, but just hit your 6,2 versus the same 6, depending upon which rules apply. (See tip 61 for other examples.) In a lifetime of blackjack playing, however, I have never once felt the need to learn such a detailed level of MBS. Please, be skeptical of any advice suggesting that you should.

All this does not imply that BS plays should not be modified in any way, regardless of what the playing conditions are. However, rather than blindly memorizing completely separate tables for every single rule variation that possibly may exist (as some books actually suggest), it is easier and much more practical to obtain some insight into why BS plays should differ from one casino to another. Armed with this understanding, you can more effortlessly adopt the appropriate MBS practically on the spot, no matter what rules happen to be in effect. Adapting your BS changes according to intelligent reasoning is far superior to blindly following some obscure table memorized by rote.

## Charity MBS

Slight changes to BS should also be implemented if you find yourself playing at a charity casino or at one of the increasingly popular native peoples' casinos. Charity casinos and most European casinos generally do not permit their dealers to take hole cards. (Instead, dealers draw their second cards only after all players have completed their hands.) You risk losing twice your original bet on doubled or split hands if the dealer draws a blackjack, since there can obviously be no "peeking" whenever he shows a T or an Ace. Therefore, it makes sense that you should not double or split any hand versus a T or Ace up-card when you play under this rule.

Similarly, it is only reasonable that you split more conservatively when playing at a casino that forbids doubling-down after splitting. Under such conditions you would not want to split your 2s or 3s against the dealer's 2s or 3s, your 6s versus a 2, nor your 4s at all. Without your opportunity to double these pairs after splitting, it is not a profitable move in the long run to break them up. The dealer simply makes too many pat hands with a 2 or 3 up-card to justify putting out any more money on these weak beginning totals. This is another example of playing to lose less; you are further ahead to simply hit your hard 4s, 6s, 8s, or 12s in these cases.

Thus, with a little thought, you can save yourself the mindless memorization of dozens of BS charts. The one presented in chapter 3 is still all you ever need to know. Suppose, for the sake of argument, you decide to play a multiple-deck session in a casino that allows you to double-down only on beginning totals of 9, 10, or 11 (in other words, no soft doubling allowed). Also imagine that no doubling after splitting is permitted. Aside from why you would play under such restrictive rules at all, the question you must ask yourself is, "What changes to my BS should I implement while playing here?"

Upon quick reflection, a twofold answer should come to mind: (1) Since no doubling is allowed after splitting, the same variations mentioned in the previous paragraph would apply, i.e., "I should not split my 2s or 3s against dealer's 2s or 3s, my 4s, or my 6s versus 2s." (2) No soft doubling suggests playing BS, as you do when you can no longer double soft totals, i.e., when your hand is comprised of more than two cards.

When playing in a casino that does not allow the surrender option, there is no need to be floored by the prospect of learning a whole new table for this occasion. Simply remember the BS chart, and just hit those four hands.

### Commonsense MBS

Common sense alone can usually indicate how to modify your playing strategies if and when memory fails. Just keep in mind that the more restrictive the rules, the more conservatively you should play. Conversely, the more liberal the rules, the more aggressive you can afford to be, especially on your splitting and doubling opportunities. The most common, fairly liberal rules found in most modern casinos allow you to play BS exactly as you learned it in chapter 3, with no modifications whatsoever. This applies to virtually all the larger casinos anywhere in the world. Remember that the worst thing that can happen to you while playing BS under absolutely terrible conditions is that you could suffer a long-term loss of up to 0.02% by sticking to your original BS rather than employing the most appropriate BS plays. In other words, don't worry about it. The difference is virtually insignificant and not worth undue concern.

Fewer than one in five of the 5% of all blackjack players who do play correctly also count cards. The noncounters who do follow proper BS will occasionally play more than one hand or follow some sort of useless bet-ranging strategy (never intentionally in ways that correspond to the TC, obviously, because they are totally unaware of what the TC is). Although these partially enlightened players always play their hands correctly and usually seem to be winning (albeit modestly), they are certainly not counters. They may even consider themselves "serious" players, since they are apt to be wagering substantial amounts of money on each hand. These players certainly enjoy the game, and perhaps they collect considerable casino comps, but how much can they really care about winning, if they haven't made the effort to learn and implement even the simplest of counting systems? They are certainly shortchanging themselves every time they sit down at the blackjack tables.

It may shock you to learn that less than one out of a hundred of all modern blackjack players is a counter who follows BS. Admittedly, it does sound incredible, especially in this day and age when the "secrets" of successful blackjack playing are so readily available. Upon reflection, however, from my own years of close observation, I would say that 1% is too high an estimate, if anything. Only rarely have I come across fellow counters, even though a professional of any sort is easily spotted when one is also tracking the cards.

If you have learned BS from chapter 3, absorbed the money management techniques from chapter 5, and mastered a practical counting system from chapter 6 and can implement it effortlessly, then you may rightly consider yourself a member of an extremely elite group. You now possess the necessary skills to win big money from the game. When next you enter a casino and see a hundred or more blackjack players crowded around the tables, know that you are likely the only player present whom the casino personnel need fear. You alone are among the less than 1% who possess the knowledge (and hence the power) to turn the tables on any casino management and actually end up winning substantial sums of money consistently. Unlike the others there, the more you play from this point onward, the more you can justifiably expect to win.

## The MBS Advantage

There is one additional, truly significant step that you can take, however, to increase your winnings even more dramatically. It is the main focus of this chapter. By adjusting or "modifying" your BS play according to what the TC happens to be, you can increase your advantage by up to three percentage points or more, depending upon how much additional information you choose to learn and how well you can apply it.

Presumably, you have had a chance to practice your blackjack skills to date, and probably have proven to yourself the value of strictly adhering to BS plays, and implementing appropriate TC wagering (see chapter 6). Obviously, you have already acquired a huge edge over any casino. Nevertheless, by using the following MBS techniques correctly, you will be providing yourself with the greatest single playing-skill advantage possible. The implementation of MBS play is primarily what distinguishes the merely good players from the truly expert. This is precisely the "secret" information currently offered players in various self-serving blackjack publications, at prices ranging from $200 to $1,000.

In chapter 3 you discovered that whenever the composition of the remaining cards to be dealt is neutral or unknown, there is an optimum or "definitive" BS, which should be followed unquestioningly in order to obtain the best long-term results. Similarly, more exhaustive computer studies have shown that as the ratio of high cards to low cards changes, certain BS plays should also change. One wins more and loses less on certain close plays because of the various probability factors involved. Some of these modifications to the BS are easy to remember, since they are so reasonable and make such good sense.

A good example to consider first might be the situation that could occur when the TC is very positive (indicating an overwhelming surplus of T's ready to appear next) and, after flipping over an Ace, the dealer asks, "Insurance, anyone?" Accepting the insurance proposition would likely be a smart decision in this case. Although BS warns against ever taking insurance, remember that BS is applicable only when the count is unknown or neutral. Since you know this TC is unusually high, BS advice is no longer completely reliable in this scenario; because you were carefully counting the cards, you realize that the odds now favor the dealer's having a T to go with the Ace. It would be foolish *not* to take advantage of this knowledge. Obviously, in certain circumstances like this, you need to modify your otherwise sound BS plays because of the additional information available to you, in this case the increased likelihood of 10-valued cards (and Aces) being readily available. Adopting slightly different BS plays according to the particular TC that happens to exist at any given moment during the game is the basic thinking behind all of the indices presented in the MBS tables in this chapter.

As it was with BS, the easiest way to learn any MBS is through understanding rather than merely memorizing the indices entirely by rote. First of all, make sure that you are completely familiar with the correct BS presented in chapter 3 and fully appreciate the reasoning behind all of its plays. If you are uncertain about any aspect of BS, stop and review it now. Unless BS is firmly established in your mind, the MBS tables that follow may appear confusing, since they only indicate where differences or exceptions in the BS plays should occur.

The next logical step is to imagine a positive Hi-Low TC of, say, +1 to +3 and how such a surplus of T's would likely affect your chances of winning, given various specific hands to play. You already understand from reading about counting-systems theory in chapter 6 why a positive count puts the odds firmly in your favor; therefore, you know that your plays can be, justifiably, a little more aggressive under these circumstances. For instance, you can double-down with somewhat more assurance that you will receive one of those most beneficial cards—the super-abundant T's—and that the dealer's hole card will more likely be a T as well.

## MBS-1

The first MBS chart below (MBS-1) shows in bold type the points at which changes should be made to normal BS plays, as the TC rises to +3 according to the corresponding index numbers listed. Various plays indicated are to be altered from regular BS plays for specific hands only if the TC is equal to or greater than those particular indices shown.

For example, if the TC is merely +1, you can see that the usual playing strategy should be modified by doubling both your 9 versus 2 and your A,8 versus 5, instead of hitting and standing respectively, as correct BS dictates for these cases. If the TC climbs to +2, however, you would then double 8 versus 6 and stand on 12 versus 2, etc., as well as follow all of the +1 indices, but not yet the +3s. When the TC does reach +3 or more, you naturally adopt appropriate playing strategy changes for all of the index numbers on the MBS-1 chart, since they stand for TC's that are equal to or greater than each number shown, and +3 obviously meets this minimum requirement.

The following abbreviations are used in all the MBS tables in this chapter:

H = Hit               P = sPlit
S = Stand             sf = soft
D = Double            An asterisk (°) indicates a questionable play.

## Modified Basic Strategy Table 1 (MBS-1)

For Hi-Low TC's from +1 to +3, in shoe games where dealers must hit soft 17s, and where doubling-down on any two cards is allowed even after splitting. No surrender offered.

| YOU have: | \|The DEALER is showing a:| | | | | | | | | |
|---|---|---|---|---|---|---|---|---|---|---|
|  | 2 | 3 | 4 | 5 | 6 | 7 | 8 | 9 | T | A |
| 5–7 | H | H | H | H | H | H | H | H | H | H |
| 8 | H | H | H | +3 | +2 | H | H | H | H | H |
| 9 | +1 | D | D | D | D | +3 | H | H | H | H |
| 10 | D | D | D | D | D | D | D | D | H | H |
| 11 | D | D | D | D | D | D | D | D | D | +1 |

(Double, if the TC equals or is greater than, and hit if the TC is less than, the integers in the section above.)

| | 2 | 3 | 4 | 5 | 6 | 7 | 8 | 9 | T | A |
|---|---|---|---|---|---|---|---|---|---|---|
| 12 | +2 | +1 | S | S | S | H | H | H | H | H |
| 13 | S | S | S | S | S | H | H | H | H | H |
| 14 | S | S | S | S | S | H | H | H | H | H |
| 15 | S | S | S | S | S | H | H | H | +3 | H |
| 16 | S | S | S | S | S | H | H | H | 0 | +3 |
| 17 | S | S | S | S | S | S | S | S | S | S |
| 18sf | S | S | S | S | S | S | S | H | H | +1* |

(Stand, if the TC equals or is greater than, but hit if the TC is less than, the integers listed in the section above.)

## The DEALER is showing a:

| YOU have: | 2 | 3 | 4 | 5 | 6 | 7 | 8 | 9 | T | A |
|---|---|---|---|---|---|---|---|---|---|---|
| A, 2 | H | H | +2 | D | D | H | H | H | H | H |
| A, 3 | H | H | +1 | D | D | H | H | H | H | H |
| A, 4 | H | H | D | D | D | H | H | H | H | H |
| A, 5 | H | +3 | D | D | D | H | H | H | H | H |
| A, 6 | +1 | D | D | D | D | H | H | H | H | H |
| A, 7 | +1 | D | D | D | D | S | S | H | H | +1* |
| A, 8 | S | S | +3 | +1 | +1 | S | S | S | S | S |
| A, 9 | S | S | S | S | S | S | S | S | S | S |

(Double, only if the TC equals or is greater than, the integers in this "soft doubling" section above. Otherwise hit or stand as BS dictates. The possible exception is A,7 versus A; stand if the TC is 1 or better.)

| | 2 | 3 | 4 | 5 | 6 | 7 | 8 | 9 | T | A |
|---|---|---|---|---|---|---|---|---|---|---|
| 2, 2 | P | P | P | P | P | P | H | H | H | H |
| 3, 3 | P | P | P | P | P | P | H | H | H | H |
| 4, 4 | H | H | +3 | D | D | H | H | H | H | H |
| 6, 6 | P | P | P | P | P | H | H | H | H | H |
| 7, 7 | P | P | P | P | P | P | H | H | H | H |
| 8, 8 | P | P | P | P | P | P | P | P | P | P |
| 9, 9 | P | P | P | P | P | +3 | P | P | S | +3 |
| A, A | P | P | P | P | P | P | P | P | P | P |

(Split, only if the TC equals or is greater than, the integers in the section above; otherwise, hit or stand as BS suggests.)

MBS-1 Notes:

1. The 16-versus-T index is 0, which requires you to stand on any positive count. This apparently contradicts BS, which requires a hit here; however, an "unknown" count is not the same as a 0 count.

2. Taking insurance is not justified with a TC of only +3.

3. If surrendering is allowed, surrender your 15 versus 9 or A when the TC = +2 or more, rather than merely hitting as BS indicates. Continue to surrender 16 versus 9, T, or A with any positive count.

4. The + signs for positive indices will not appear on subsequent tables. The negative TC's will retain minus signs in front of them in order to distinguish between these two different types of integers.

If you plan to learn only a bit of MBS, for whatever your reasons, then the MBS-1 chart shown above should certainly be it. First of all, knowing the correct plays to make when the count is positive is much more important than when the count is negative. This is true because you will have more money on the table with positive counts, and therefore stand to win or lose more on these hands. (Very conservative players do not play at all unless the count is positive.) Second, learning the correct indices for TC's up to +3 includes most of the positive ranges that you are apt to encounter in a shoe game.

## MBS-2

If you expand the TC range downward to include the −3 integers, as shown on the next table (MBS-2), then you will have at your disposal the perfect playing strategies for over 86% of the TC's that normally occur within any six-deck shoe game. As mentioned in chapter 4, the TC stays within the limits of +3 and −3 approximately 86.6% of the time. Therefore, if you have absorbed the MBS-1 information without too much difficulty, you are well advised to study the next chart, since you will probably find yourself playing with a slightly negative count from time to time, and knowing the proper MBS plays within this TC range will certainly save you money in those instances.

### Modified Basic Strategy Table 2 (MBS-2)

For Hi-Low TC's from −3 to +3, in shoe games where dealers must hit soft 17s, and where doubling-down on any two cards is allowed even after splitting. No surrender offered.

|  | The DEALER is showing a: | | | | | | | | | |
|---|---|---|---|---|---|---|---|---|---|---|
| **YOU have:** | 2 | 3 | 4 | 5 | 6 | 7 | 8 | 9 | T | A |
| 5–7 | H | H | H | H | H | H | H | H | H | H |
| 8 | H | H | H | 3 | 2 | H | H | H | H | H |
| 9 | I | −I | −2 | D | D | 3 | H | H | H | H |
| 10 | D | D | D | D | D | D | D | −I | H | H |
| 11 | D | D | D | D | D | D | D | D | −3 | I |

(Double, if the TC equals or is greater than, and hit if the TC is less than, the integers in the section above.)

**The DEALER is showing a:**

| YOU have: | 2 | 3 | 4 | 5 | 6 | 7 | 8 | 9 | T | A |
|---|---|---|---|---|---|---|---|---|---|---|
| 12 | 2 | 1 | 0 | −1 | −2 | H | H | H | H | H |
| 13 | −1 | −2 | S | S | S | H | H | H | H | H |
| 14 | −3 | S | S | S | S | H | H | H | H | H |
| 15 | S | S | S | S | S | H | H | H | 3 | H |
| 16 | S | S | S | S | S | H | H | H | 0 | 3 |
| 17+ | S | S | S | S | S | S | S | S | S | S |
| 18sf | S | S | S | S | S | S | S | H | H | 1* |

(Stand, if the TC equals or is greater than, but hit if the TC is less than, the integers listed in the section above.)

| | 2 | 3 | 4 | 5 | 6 | 7 | 8 | 9 | T | A |
|---|---|---|---|---|---|---|---|---|---|---|
| A, 2 | H | H | 2 | −1 | −2 | H | H | H | H | H |
| A, 3 | H | H | 1 | −2 | D | H | H | H | H | H |
| A, 4 | H | H | −1 | D | D | H | H | H | H | H |
| A, 5 | H | 3 | −1 | D | D | H | H | H | H | H |
| A, 6 | 1 | −2 | D | D | D | H | H | H | H | H |
| A, 7 | 1 | −1 | D | D | D | S | S | H | H | 1* |
| A, 8 | S | S | 3 | 1 | 1 | S | S | S | S | S |
| A, 9 | S | S | S | S | S | S | S | S | S | S |

(Double, only if the TC equals or is greater than the integers in this "soft doubling" section above; otherwise hit or stand as BS dictates. The possible exception is A,7 versus A; stand if the TC is 1 or better.)

| | 2 | 3 | 4 | 5 | 6 | 7 | 8 | 9 | T | A |
|---|---|---|---|---|---|---|---|---|---|---|
| 2, 2 | P | P | P | P | P | P | H | H | H | H |
| 3, 3 | −2 | P | P | P | P | P | H | H | H | H |
| 4, 4 | H | H | 3 | −1 | −2 | H | H | H | H | H |
| 6, 6 | −1 | P | P | P | P | H | H | H | H | H |
| 7, 7 | P | P | P | P | P | P | H | H | H | H |
| 8, 8 | P | P | P | P | P | P | P | P | P | P |
| 9, 9 | −2 | −3 | P | P | P | 3 | P | P | S | 3 |
| A, A | P | P | P | P | P | P | P | P | P | P |

(Split, only if the TC equals or is greater than, the shown in the section above; otherwise, hit or stand as BS suggests.)

MBS-2 Notes

1. Taking insurance is not justified with a TC of only + 3.

2. If surrendering is allowed, surrender your 15 versus 9 or A when the TC = 2 or more. Also surrender 16 versus 9, T, or A with any positive count.

3. Splitting 4s is always preferable to doubling the 8, unless doubling after splitting is not allowed.

4. Soft 18 (shown as "18sf" above) is often obtained after doubling is no longer an option. It is included here, since it is the only soft total that has a potential MBS.

Perhaps an easier way to grasp the significance of the MBS integers shown on these charts is to view them simply as "cutoff" points, beyond which correct playing decisions depart from the regular "tried and true" BS. The numbers simply represent the "limits" where BS no longer properly applies.

For those readers who are not very mathematically inclined, let's quickly review the BS play changes indicated on the MBS-2 chart above, section by section. This concept is far too important to risk any confusion. Once you are completely at ease interpreting the information presented on the table above, reading subsequent MBS charts will be more beneficial, because they will be easily understood and more quickly absorbed. Those readers who are having no difficulty grasping these MBS concepts may decide to skip ahead to the MBS-4 chart.

## The DEALER is showing a:

| YOU have: | 2 | 3 | 4 | 5 | 6 | 7 | 8 | 9 | T | A |
|-----------|---|---|---|---|---|---|---|---|---|---|
| 8 | H | H | H | 3 | 2 | H | H | H | H | H |
| 9 | I | −I | −2 | D | D | 3 | H | H | H | H |
| 10 | D | D | D | D | D | D | D | −I | H | H |
| 11 | D | D | D | D | D | D | D | D | −3 | I |

When you receive a total of 8 against the dealer's 5 or 6, BS tells you to simply hit it. However, if you know that the TC is + 3 or more, you can gain the advantage of a bonus bet in these two cases by doubling-down. You are more than likely to end up with an 18, while the dealer is even more apt to bust, since she will be forced to add at least two more draws to the stiff 5 or 6 up-cards. The index "2" means that + 2 is the "point of departure" from BS. If the TC = + 2 or more, double your 8 versus a 6.

When the TC is less than +2, you revert to BS and just take a hit. Similarly, the TC must be +3 or more before doubling your 8 against a 5 is justified.

The same reasoning applies to your 9 versus a 2 or a 7. Double-down when the TC is +1 or more and +3 or more, respectively. Otherwise simply hit these hands, as you would playing normal BS.

The "−1" index for your 9 versus 3 means that you should *not* double if the TC is less than −1, but abide by BS if the TC equals or is greater than −1. Similarly, the "−2" index for your 9 versus 4 means that you should *not* double-down if the TC is less than −2, but *do* follow BS as long as the TC is −2 or higher.

You must remember, of course, that −1 is more than −2. Thinking about subzero temperatures on a thermometer scale can help clear up any difficulty you may be experiencing in ranking negative integers. For example, a reading of −1 degree on a thermometer is "one below zero," which is a higher temperature, i.e., more heat, than −2 degrees. Similarly, a TC of −1 is greater than −2.

The cutoff points indicated by these negative indices make good sense, because you would not want to risk receiving small cards after doubling-down, especially when the dealer's chances of drawing pat hands are actually increased because of the weaker TC's (which indicate a superabundance of low-ranking cards available). Likewise, doubling your 10 versus 9 is not wise if the TC is less than −1, since there is a better chance you will not receive a T.

Doubling your 11 versus A is advisable now, since your chances of getting 21 are somewhat increased with a TC of +1 or more. The "−3" means that you should depart from BS if the TC is less than −3, because the odds of your drawing a low card on your double would be too great.

### The DEALER is showing a:

| YOU have: | 2 | 3 | 4 | 5 | 6 | 7 | 8 | 9 | T | A |
|---|---|---|---|---|---|---|---|---|---|---|
| 12 | 2 | 1 | 0 | −1 | −2 | H | H | H | H | H |
| 13 | −1 | −2 | S | S | S | H | H | H | H | H |
| 14 | −3 | S | S | S | S | H | H | H | H | H |
| 15 | S | S | S | S | S | H | H | H | 3 | H |
| 16 | S | S | S | S | S | H | H | H | 0 | 3 |
| 18sf | S | S | S | S | S | S | S | H | H | 1* |

When you draw a 12 versus 2 or 3, BS dictates taking a hit, but when the TC's reach +2 and +1 respectively, correct MBS requires you to stand. Although the chance of the dealer's busting is greater with these counts, so is yours! It is no longer worth taking the chance of trying to improve your hard 12, as it was when the count was neutral or unknown. The "0" index for 12 versus 4 means to stand on *any* positive RC, but hit for *any* negative RC. "−1" and "−2" for the 5 and 6 indices tells you to stick with the BS unless the TC drops below −1 or −2 respectively, in which case you would obviously hit.

Hit your 13 versus a 2 or 3 when the TC is lower than the table numbers of −1 and −2 respectively. Similarly, 14 versus 2 justifies a hit if the TC is less than 3. You are more apt to improve your stiff totals in these cases, rather than bust, when the counts are negative.

With surrendering not being offered as an option, stand with a 15 versus T if the TC is +3 or more. Also, a 16 versus T or A does not warrant a hit if the TC's are better than 0 and +3 respectively. With these losing hands, in such situations your best option is to stand and hope the dealer busts because of the extra T's that are ready and waiting to appear.

### The DEALER is showing a:

| YOU have: | 2 | 3 | 4 | 5 | 6 | 7 | 8 | 9 | T | A |
|---|---|---|---|---|---|---|---|---|---|---|
| A, 2 | H | H | 2 | −1 | −2 | H | H | H | H | H |
| A, 3 | H | H | 1 | −2 | D | H | H | H | H | H |
| A, 4 | H | H | −1 | D | D | H | H | H | H | H |
| A, 5 | H | 3 | −2 | D | D | H | H | H | H | H |
| A, 6 | 1 | −2 | D | D | D | H | H | H | H | H |
| A, 7 | 1 | −1 | D | D | D | S | S | H | H | 1* |
| A, 8 | S | S | 3 | 1 | 1 | S | S | S | S | S |

All of the numbers in this section, except one, indicate that a double-down is required if the TC equals, or is greater than the indices shown. The sole exception is the case of A,7 versus A. It is sometimes recommended to stand (rather than take a hit as BS dictates) with any soft 18 versus an Ace when the TC is +1 or better. Although this advice is not unanimously accepted as the correct strategy, its merit is definitely worth considering. The argument is basically this: As the TC increases, the likelihood of your improving an 18 total diminishes, since you will probably just turn your hand from soft to hard. The dealer must have a small card in the hole (smaller than a T at least) and may be forced to draw an additional card to it, thereby creating a greater chance of breaking.

Since I can find no definitive answer regarding this particular situation from extant sources, it must be left up to you to make your own decision. Whichever way you decide to play this hand, though, be consistent. Don't worry about it much. Even if you choose the "wrong" play, your losses over time will be negligible. It is presently an arbitrary call, of which players should be aware, and I would welcome proof one way or the other so that future printings of this publication could provide unambiguous advice regarding this particular circumstance.

| | **The DEALER is showing a:** | | | | | | | | | |
|---|---|---|---|---|---|---|---|---|---|---|
| **YOU have:** | **2** | **3** | **4** | **5** | **6** | **7** | **8** | **9** | **T** | **A** |
| 3, 3 | −2 | P | P | P | P | P | H | H | H | H |
| 4, 4 | H | H | 3 | −1 | −2 | H | H | H | H | H |
| 6, 6 | −1 | P | P | P | P | H | H | H | H | H |
| 9, 9 | −2 | −3 | P | P | P | 3 | P | P | S | 3 |

Do not split if the TC is less than the table numbers shown in this section. Split only if the TC equals or is greater than the appropriate indices indicated. Otherwise follow BS rules for the remaining splits.

## MBS-3

The following table (MBS-3) is probably enough MBS for most players to learn. It shows all the correct playing indices for TC's that range from −5 to +5, and this represents over 95% of all TC's normally encountered in any six-deck shoe game.

### Modified Basic Strategy Table 3 (MBS-3)

For Hi-Low TC's from −5 to +5, in shoe games where dealers hit soft 17s and where doubling-down on any two cards is allowed even after splitting. No surrender offered.

| YOU have: | The **DEALER** is showing a: | | | | | | | | | |
|---|---|---|---|---|---|---|---|---|---|---|
| | **2** | **3** | **4** | **5** | **6** | **7** | **8** | **9** | **T** | **A** |
| 8 | H | H | 5 | 3 | 2 | H | H | H | H | H |
| 9 | 1 | −1 | −2 | −4 | −5 | 3 | H | H | H | H |
| 10 | D | D | D | D | D | D | −4 | −1 | 4 | 4 |
| 11 | D | D | D | D | D | D | D | −4 | −3 | 1 |

(Double, if the TC equals or is greater than, and hit if the TC is less than, the integers in the section above.)

| | **2** | **3** | **4** | **5** | **6** | **7** | **8** | **9** | **T** | **A** |
|---|---|---|---|---|---|---|---|---|---|---|
| 12 | 2 | 1 | 0 | −1 | −2 | H | H | H | H | H |
| 13 | −1 | −2 | −4 | −5 | −5 | H | H | H | H | H |
| 14 | −3 | −4 | −5 | S | S | H | H | H | H | H |
| 15 | S | S | S | S | S | H | H | H | 3 | 5 |
| 16 | S | S | S | S | S | H | H | 4 | 0 | 3 |
| 17 | S | S | S | S | S | S | S | S | S | −5 |
| 18sf | S | S | S | S | S | S | S | H | H | 1* |

(Stand, if the TC equals or is greater than, but hit if the TC is less than, the integers in the section above.)

| | **2** | **3** | **4** | **5** | **6** | **7** | **8** | **9** | **T** | **A** |
|---|---|---|---|---|---|---|---|---|---|---|
| A, 2 | H | H | 2 | −1 | −2 | H | H | H | H | H |
| A, 3 | H | H | 1 | −2 | −4 | H | H | H | H | H |
| A, 4 | H | 5 | −1 | −4 | D | H | H | H | H | H |
| A, 5 | H | 3 | −2 | −5 | D | H | H | H | H | H |
| A, 6 | 1 | −2 | −5 | D | D | H | H | H | H | H |
| A, 7 | 1 | −1 | −5 | D | D | S | S | H | H | 1* |
| A, 8 | S | 5 | 3 | 1 | 1 | S | S | S | S | S |
| A, 9 | S | S | S | 5 | 5 | S | S | S | S | S |

(Double, only if the TC equals or is greater than the integers in this "soft doubling" section above. Otherwise hit or stand as BS dictates. The exception is A,7 versus A; stand if the TC is 1 or better.)

**The DEALER is showing a:**

| 'OU have: | 2 | 3 | 4 | 5 | 6 | 7 | 8 | 9 | T | A |
|---|---|---|---|---|---|---|---|---|---|---|
| 2 | −4 | −5 | P | P | P | P | H | H | H | H |
| 3, 3 | −2 | −5 | P | P | P | P | H | H | H | H |
| 4, 4 | H | H | 3 | −1 | −2 | H | H | H | H | H |
| 6, 6 | −1 | −3 | −4 | P | P | H | H | H | H | H |
| 7, 7 | P | P | P | P | P | P | H | H | H | H |
| 8, 8 | P | P | P | P | P | P | P | P | P | P |
| 9, 9 | −2 | −3 | −5 | −5 | P | 3 | P | P | S | 3 |
| T, T | S | S | S | 5 | 4 | S | S | S | S | S |
| A, A | P | P | P | P | P | P | P | P | P | −5 |

(Split, only if the TC equals or is greater than the integers shown in the section above.)

MBS-3 Notes

    1. With a TC of 4 or more, insurance is justified.

    2. If surrendering is allowed: (a) Surrender 14 versus 10 if the TC = 3 or more, and 14 versus A if the TC = 5 or more. (b) Surrender your 15 versus 9 or A when the TC = 2 or more, and 15 versus T if the TC is at all positive. (c) Surrender 16 versus 9, T, or A with any positive count, and 16 (but not 8,8) versus 8 if the TC = 4 or more.

    3. Splitting 4s is always preferable to doubling the 8, unless doubling after splitting is not allowed.

    4. Notice that T's are to be split sometimes, contrary to popular belief. Do not resplit T's, however, if the TC falls below the respective integers shown because of cards drawn to a previous split.

    5. *Never* split 5s regardless of how high the TC may climb.

    6. Soft 18 (listed as "18sf" above) is often obtained after doubling is no longer an option. It is included here, since it is the only soft total that has a potential MBS, depending upon which sources are accepted. Only Revere, Humble, and Cooper advise players to stand with A,7 (or any soft 18) versus an Ace when the TC is 1 or more; therefore, this play must be considered somewhat questionable.

With negative TC's of −5 or less, it is always interesting to watch noncounting players' reactions as their splits and double-downs result in extremely weak final totals—"stiffs" more often than not. The players' disgust is only exacerbated by the fact that the dealers seem to more consistently end up with pat hands (not surprising, with such a surplus of small cards eager to pop out of the shoe), perhaps after originally showing only lowly 5s or 6s. Even noncounters realize that a dealer will normally bust when starting with these poor up-cards, so they are prematurely anticipating their winnings; imagine their incredible chagrin as the dealer proceeds to draw strong totals, often 20s or 21s. What these unfortunate folk do not know is that, with only two decks remaining, a −5 count means that there are ten more small cards than big ones available to be dealt. Rather than being shocked at their resultant stiff hands and the pat hands of the dealers, the players should be much more surprised if anything other than these results occurred. Then again, they couldn't possibly know what is apt to happen at such times, being completely unaware of the count as they are.

If you are not prepared to commit the whole MBS-3 table to memory, estimating what the numbers might be and playing accordingly is better than remaining totally ignorant of the best plays. You will still be making money from the game while you gradually increase your MBS repertoire. As with most things in life, expect to get out of these MBS charts what you are willing to put into them. In actual fact, you will gain many more rewards than merely the time and energy spent in learning these MBS integers would seem to justify.

A short visit to your respective men's or ladies' room when the TC is very bad will obviously save you money, and it is much easier than learning a myriad of correct negative-TC MBS plays. However, if you intend to sit down and play continuously through shoe after shoe regardless of the count, you may be wise to obtain at least a passing acquaintance with the more complete MBS-4 chart that follows. By understanding the reasoning behind the indices shown there, you will soon be able to approximate them fairly accurately, even if you do not learn them 100%.

The larger the integers that appear upon MBS tables, the less practical use they are to you, since TC's reach these figures so rarely. Strangely enough, the more decks used, the more apt the TC's are to remain within narrower limits. Simply abiding by BS, instead of learning and implementing 100% correct MBS for bigger numbers encountered on a chart, represents only a very small percentage loss to the player. For example, knowing that you should double a two-card total of 5 against the dealer's 3 when the TC = 20 or more is obviously of limited value. One can expect to be in this situation approximately once every 1.6 million hands. For the vast majority of players, it is not worth exerting the effort to memorize such extreme TC ranges.

## MBS-4

For those very serious readers who may be interested, however, a fairly extensive MBS-4 table is included below. It was compiled by collating information from a wide range of reputable sources. Where discrepancies between various tables occured, the integers finally chosen were "averaged" to arrive at the compromised figures shown on the chart. A conscious effort was made to err on the "conservative" side whenever possible. Keep in mind that absolute accuracy is never possible when dealing with MBS plays at any time, since they are necessarily just an "estimate" at best. After all, TC's can only be determined by "guessing" how many unseen decks remain in the shoe.

In any case, this MBS-4 table is definitely the most comprehensive amalgamation of all MBS advice presently available from all known blackjack literature for Hi-Low TC's ranging between −20 and +20. The reader may be completely assured that every effort was exerted to make this the most reliable MBS data that could reasonably be required by any conscientious blackjack player today.

Nevertheless, for even further precise plays, see Wong's *Professional Blackjack,* which includes tables showing such minutiae as how every specific two-card total should be played in order to wring out the last possible drop of advantage for the dedicated professional. For example, playing in a four-deck shoe game in which the dealer hits soft 17, if your 7 consists of 4,3 you should double versus a 4 when the TC is 11 or more, but if your 7 is comprised of 5,2 then a TC of at least 12 is required before the double is warranted. Again, keep in mind that this knowledge would be useful less than once every 1.6 million hands on average. Even for the most serious of players, learning such a sophisticated level of MBS play is impossible to justify, but the reader should be aware that the research has been done and that the information is available, just in case.

## Modified Basic Strategy Table 4 (MBS-4)

For Hi-Low TC's in shoe games where dealers must hit soft 17s, and where doubling-down on any two cards is allowed even after splitting. No surrender offered.

### The DEALER is showing a:

| YOU have: | 2 | 3 | 4 | 5 | 6 | 7 | 8 | 9 | T | A |
|---|---|---|---|---|---|---|---|---|---|---|
| 5 | H | 20 | 15 | 12 | 13 | H | H | H | H | H |
| 6 | H | 20 | 15 | 11 | 12 | H | H | H | H | H |
| 7 | H | 16 | 12 | 9 | 8 | H | H | H | H | H |
| 8 | 13 | 9 | 5 | 3 | 2 | 14 | H | H | H | H |
| 9 | 1 | −1 | −2 | −4 | −5 | 3 | 7 | H | H | H |
| 10 | −9 | −10 | −11 | −12 | −14 | −7 | −4 | −1 | 4 | 4 |
| 11 | −12 | −13 | −14 | −15 | −17 | −10 | −7 | −4 | −3 | 1 |

(Double, if the TC equals or is greater than, and hit if the TC is less than, the integers in the section above.)

| | 2 | 3 | 4 | 5 | 6 | 7 | 8 | 9 | T | A |
|---|---|---|---|---|---|---|---|---|---|---|
| 12 | 2 | 1 | 0 | −1 | −2 | H | H | H | H | H |
| 13 | −1 | −2 | −4 | −5 | −5 | H | H | H | H | 15 |
| 14 | −3 | −4 | −5 | −8 | −10 | 17 | H | H | H | 9 |
| 15 | −6 | −8 | −9 | −10 | −12 | 10 | 10 | 8 | 3 | 5 |
| 16 | −10 | −11 | −12 | −13 | −15 | 9 | 7 | 4 | 0 | 3 |
| 17 | S | S | S | S | S | S | S | S | S | −5 |
| 18sf | −15 | −16 | −15 | −16 | −16 | S | −16 | H | H | 1* |

(Stand, if the TC equals or is greater than, but hit if the TC is less than, the integers in the section above.)

| | 2 | 3 | 4 | 5 | 6 | 7 | 8 | 9 | T | A |
|---|---|---|---|---|---|---|---|---|---|---|
| A, 2 | 12 | 7 | 2 | −1 | −2 | H | H | H | H | H |
| A, 3 | 14 | 6 | 1 | −2 | −4 | H | H | H | H | H |
| A, 4 | 18 | 5 | −1 | −4 | −11 | H | H | H | H | H |
| A, 5 | 15 | 3 | −2 | −5 | −14 | H | H | H | H | H |
| A, 6 | 1 | −2 | −5 | −10 | −15 | 11* | H | H | H | H |
| A, 7 | 1 | −1 | −5 | −9 | −14 | 20 | S | H | H | (1*) |
| A, 8 | 8 | 5 | 3 | 1 | 1 | 17 | S | S | S | S |
| A, 9 | 10 | 8 | 6 | 5 | 5 | 14 | S | S | S | S |

(Double, only if the TC equals or is greater than the integers shown in this "soft doubling" section; otherwise, hit or stand as BS dictates. The possible exception is A,7 versus A; stand if the TC is 1 or better.)

**The DEALER is showing a:**

| YOU have: | 2 | 3 | 4 | 5 | 6 | 7 | 8 | 9 | T | A |
|-----------|-----|-----|-----|-----|-----|-----|-----|-----|-----|-----|
| 2, 2 | −4 | −5 | −8 | −10 | −12 | −20 | 6 | H | H | H |
| 3, 3 | −2 | −5 | −8 | −10 | −12 | −20 | 4 | H | H | H |
| 4, 4 | 14 | 6 | 3 | −1 | −2 | H | H | H | H | H |
| 6, 6 | −1 | −3 | −4 | −6 | −9 | H | H | H | H | H |
| 7, 7 | −11 | −12 | −14 | −15 | −17 | −20 | H | H | H | H |
| 8, 8 | P | P | P | P | P | P | P | P | (8) | −2 |
| 9, 9 | −2 | −3 | −5 | −5 | −6 | 3 | −9 | −10 | S | 3 |
| T, T | 11 | 8 | 6 | 5 | 4 | 13 | 20 | S | S | S |
| A, A | −12 | −13 | −14 | −14 | −15 | −10 | −9 | −8 | −9 | −5 |

(Split, only if the TC equals or is greater than the integers in the section above. Otherwise hit or stand as BS dictates. The one exception: Do *not* split 8s versus T if the TC is 8 or more; when surrender is not an option, just stand instead.)

MBS-4 Notes

1. Only Revere, Humble, and Cooper advise players to stand with A,7 (or any soft 18) versus an Ace when the TC is 1 or more. Cardoza alone suggests doubling A,6 versus 7 if the TC = 11 or more. Although these plays are reasonable and should likely be followed, they are listed as "questionable" since there is no corroborating data to support their claims.

2. Another obscure blackjack writer, Silberstang, recommends standing with A,7 or 7,7 versus 10 with any positive count, but his "proof" is completely unsubstantiated, and since these plays seem somewhat less rational they should probably be ignored.

3. Flat betting (same-sized bet every time) even while playing proper MBS will not win you more money in the long run than merely correct TC bet-ranging played with ordinary BS, unless you are being somewhat conservative and playing, for example, *only* with TC's of +3 or more (see Griffen's *Theory of Blackjack*). Therefore, to gain the full advantage of

your MBS knowledge, you must also combine it with the TC bet-ranging outlined in chapter 6.

4. It should be noted that when the TC is 4 or more, insurance is generally a good bet; however, in shoe games where many Aces may have already appeared (thereby canceling a similar number of small cards in the count), a TC of 3 or less can often justify taking advantage of the insurance proposition. Employing Thorp's Ten-count system precisely is the only way to be absolutely sure of when accepting the insurance wager is a good bet.

## Modified Basic Strategy Chart 5 (MBS-5)

The table below indicates when to surrender. Since *no* casinos offer "early" surrender any more, surrender always means "late" surrender nowadays. When offered, TC surrendering nearly always takes precedence over every other possible play. More and more casinos are allowing the surrender option, since it is usually an extra moneymaker for them when used by unknowledgeable players.

| | The DEALER is showing a: | | | | |
|---|---|---|---|---|---|
| **YOU have:** | 7 | 8 | 9 | T | A |
| 5 | H | H | H | 17 | H |
| 6 | H | H | 20 | 18 | H |
| 7 | H | H | H | 19 | H |
| 12 | H | H | 20 | 14 | H |
| 13 | H | 19 | 13 | 7 | H |
| 14 | 16 | 12 | 6 | 3 | 5 |
| 15 | 10 | 6 | 2 | 0 | 2 |
| 16 (not 8s) | 12 | 4 | 0 | −2 | −1 |
| 17 | S | S | 13 | 12 | S |

(Surrender only if the TC equals or is greater than the integers shown above. Otherwise follow the usual MBS plays.)

MBS-5 Notes
1. Player totals of 5, 6, and 7 include soft totals.
2. The sole exception to surrender precedence is 8,8: (i) 8s versus 9

always requires a split no matter what the TC is; (ii) 8s versus T are to
be surrendered *only* if the TC equals or is greater than 8 (see MBS-4);
(iii) 8s versus A should be surrendered rather than split *only* when the
TC is less than −2 (see MBS-4).

Many beginning players worry, completely unnecessarily, that they
do not have 100% recollection of all the correct MBS indices at their
immediate disposal. It is not at all vital regardless of which MBS chart
you have mastered, for three main reasons:

1. All MBS plays are just educated guesses; after all, TC's are merely
   estimates at best.
2. Playing MBS according to strategy numbers that are close, but not
   precisely the correct indices results in such extremely minor
   losses that they may truly be considered negligible.
3. You will still be winning money by simply following BS alone
   while you continue to learn the MBS indices in more detail.

The most important thing that any player can achieve from this
chapter is an understanding of the MBS principles involved. Only then
can one's intuition or "gut feelings" be a trusted guide through
uncertain plays. However, the best rule of thumb is: *Never go against
BS unless you have a good reason!* When you know that you should, use
your existing knowledge of the MBS charts, to whatever degree of
proficiency you have attained, in order to make the most out of every
situation by consistently following only intelligent playing decisions.

## MBS Practice Exercises

Learning MBS is a slow, tedious process, but well worth the effort. Try
to be patient with yourself. The following exercises were specially
designed for your MBS practice. In each case, the relevant Hi-Low TC
is listed. Always assume that you are playing shoe games that follow the
rules normally found, but where surrender is not allowed unless
indicated.

In each exercise, carefully consider your various hands versus the up-cards shown in order to determine the correct plays as presented on the MBS-4 chart, according to the appropriate TC. The exercises get progressively more difficult, so that you may more easily advance to your desired level of MBS expertise. Remember that you modify basic playing strategy *only* when warranted by the TC; otherwise the correct play is always determined by BS alone. For most efficient learning, cover the answers until after you have decided upon your play in each case. Revealing the correct response then tends to reinforce your learning immediately.

Practice doing the exercises forward and backward, until you can achieve 100% accuracy at the level of your choice. It is strongly recommended that MBS exercises G and H be mastered as well, since the popular surrender option is becoming much more widespread and can save you a bundle when used properly.

The following abbreviations continue to be used in the exercises:

H = Hit          D = Double-down
S = Stand        G = Give up (i.e., surrender)
P = sPlit

## MBS Practice Exercise A
### When the TC = +1, and no surrender offered

| Your Hand | Up-card | BS | Your Hand | Up-card | BS |
|-----------|---------|-----|-----------|---------|-----|
| 7, 5 | 3 | S | 5, 3 | 4 | H |
| 2, 7 | 2 | D | 9, 7 | T | S |
| A, 3 | 4 | D | 8, 8 | 9 | P |
| 2, A | 7 | H | 5, 6 | A | D |
| A, 8 | 6 | D | 5, 5 | A | H |
| 6, 6 | 4 | P | 8, 4 | 4 | S |
| A, 6 | 2 | D | 7, A | 2 | D |
| 4, 8 | 2 | H | A, 2 | 4 | H |
| T, 5 | T | H | 6, T | A | H |
| A, 8 | 5 | D | A, 7 | A | S |

## MBS Practice Exercise B
### When the TC = −1, and no surrender offered

| Your Hand | Up-card | BS | Your Hand | Up-card | BS |
|-----------|---------|----|-----------|---------|----|
| 6, 7 | 2 | S | 4, 5 | 3 | D |
| 9, 3 | 4 | H | A, 7 | A | H |
| T, 6 | T | H | 8, A | 6 | S |
| 7, A | 2 | S | 2, 6 | 6 | H |
| 5, 5 | 2 | D | 7, A | 5 | D |
| T, 5 | 9 | H | 6, 6 | 5 | P |
| A, 4 | 5 | D | A, 2 | 7 | H |
| T, T | 6 | S | 2, 2 | 5 | P |
| 7, 3 | 6 | D | 8, 3 | 5 | D |
| A, 7 | 4 | D | 9, 3 | 2 | H |

## MBS Practice Exercise C-1
### When the TC = +3, and no surrender offered

| Your Hand | Up-card | BS | Your Hand | Up-card | BS |
|-----------|---------|----|-----------|---------|----|
| 3, 5 | 5 | D | 8, 4 | 2 | S |
| 4, 4 | 3 | P | A, 8 | 3 | S |
| 2, 7 | 7 | D | 5, A | 3 | D |
| A, 8 | 4 | D | 9, 9 | 7 | P |
| 9, 9 | A | P | 5, 3 | 6 | D |
| 2, T | 2 | S | 6, 5 | A | D |
| A, 2 | 4 | D | T, T | 6 | S |
| T, 5 | T | D | 6, T | A | S |
| A, A | A | P | 4, 5 | 2 | D |
| 7, 5 | 3 | S | A, 7 | 2 | D |

## MBS Practice Exercise C-2
## When the TC = +3, and no surrender offered

| Your Hand | Up-card | BS | Your Hand | Up-card | BS |
|-----------|---------|----|-----------|---------|----|
| 3, 5 | 5 | D | 8, 4 | 2 | S |
| A, 4 | 5 | D | A, 2 | 7 | H |
| 9, 7 | A | S | 5, 5 | A | H |
| 6, 6 | 4 | P | 8, 4 | 4 | S |
| A, 6 | 2 | D | 7, A | 2 | D |
| 5, A | 3 | D | A, 8 | 4 | D |
| 9, 9 | 7 | P | 9, 9 | A | P |
| T, T | 6 | S | 7, 9 | 9 | H |
| A, 7 | 4 | D | 9, 3 | 2 | S |
| 7, 5 | 3 | S | A, 9 | 6 | S |

## MBS Practice Exercise D
## When the TC = −3, and no surrender offered

| Your Hand | Up-card | BS | Your Hand | Up-card | BS |
|-----------|---------|----|-----------|---------|----|
| 5, 4 | 5 | D | 4, 5 | 4 | H |
| 2, 8 | 8 | D | 5, 5 | 9 | H |
| T, 4 | 2 | S | 6, 5 | T | D |
| A, 3 | 5 | H | 3, A | 6 | D |
| 4, A | 5 | D | 8, 8 | A | H |
| 3, 3 | 2 | H | 6, 6 | 3 | P |
| 7, 2 | 3 | H | 6, 4 | 9 | H |
| 9, 9 | 2 | S | 9, 9 | 3 | P |
| 8, 8 | T | P | A, 7 | 3 | S |
| 7, A | 4 | D | A, 5 | 4 | H |

## MBS Practice Exercise E
### When the TC = +5, and no surrender offered

| Your Hand | Up-card | BS | Your Hand | Up-card | BS |
|-----------|---------|----|-----------|---------|----|
| 2, 8 | A | D | 2, 6 | 4 | D |
| 3, 4 | 6 | H | T, 6 | 9 | S |
| A, 7 | A | S | T, T | 5 | P |
| A, 9 | 5 | D | 8, 4 | 2 | S |
| 3, 5 | 4 | D | 5, T | A | S |
| 4, A | 3 | D | A, 8 | 3 | D |
| A, 7 | A | S | 6, 4 | T | D |
| 7, 2 | 8 | H | A, 3 | 3 | H |
| A, 7 | 7 | S | 9, A | 6 | D |
| 9, 9 | A | P | A, 5 | 3 | D |

## MBS Practice Exercise F
### When the TC = −5, and no surrender offered

| Your Hand | Up-card | BS | Your Hand | Up-card | BS |
|-----------|---------|----|-----------|---------|----|
| 9, 9 | 4 | P | 9, 9 | 5 | P |
| 2, 7 | 6 | D | 5, 6 | 9 | H |
| T, 2 | 6 | H | 3, T | 5 | S |
| A, 5 | 5 | D | 5, A | 4 | H |
| 6, 6 | 5 | P | 6, 6 | 4 | H |
| 2, 2 | 3 | P | 2, 2 | 2 | H |
| T, 3 | 6 | S | 4, T | 3 | H |
| 4, T | 4 | S | T, 7 | A | S |
| A, 6 | 4 | D | A, 2 | 6 | H |
| 9, 9 | 6 | P | 4, 4 | 6 | H |

## MBS Practice Exercise G
### When the TC = +5, and surrendering *is* offered

| Your Hand | Up-card | BS | Your Hand | Up-card | BS |
|-----------|---------|-----|-----------|---------|-----|
| 4, T | T | G | T, 5 | 9 | G |
| 8, 8 | 9 | P | 7, 8 | 8 | H |
| 8, 8 | A | P | T, 7 | A | S |
| 9, 7 | 9 | G | 7, 7 | T | G |
| 5, T | T | G | T, 6 | A | G |
| 6, T | 8 | G | A, 9 | 5 | D |
| 6, 7 | A | H | 7, 7 | A | G |
| 8, 8 | T | P | 9, 7 | A | G |
| T, 4 | A | G | T, 5 | 7 | H |
| 8, 8 | 8 | G | 5, T | A | G |

## MBS Practice Exercise H
### When the TC = −5 and surrender *is* offered

| Your Hand | Up-card | BS | Your Hand | Up-card | BS |
|-----------|---------|-----|-----------|---------|-----|
| 8, 8 | T | P | T, 6 | T | H |
| 4, T | A | H | 8, 8 | 9 | P |
| T, 5 | T | H | 7, T | A | S |
| T, 3 | A | H | 8, 8 | A | G |
| 9, 9 | 6 | P | T, 3 | 4 | H |
| 9, 7 | 8 | H | 8, 8 | 8 | P |
| 6, T | T | H | 6, T | 9 | H |
| 7, 8 | 9 | H | 8, 8 | A | G |
| T, 6 | A | H | 7, 8 | A | H |
| T, 4 | T | H | T, 7 | A | S |

Congratulations! Rather than merely thinking of yourself as an expert card-counter and successful player, having mastered MBS play you can now rightly consider yourself as much of a threat to the casinos as that most dreaded of patrons—the blackjack professional. You will, no doubt, proceed to make even more money from the game, because "good fortune" is now sure to accompany you to any blackjack table in the world. It's a strange fact that the more one knows about this game, the "luckier" one tends to be. So, good luck! You've certainly earned it!

# 8

# 101 Playing Tips

The following general blackjack tips are meant to shore up the playing strategies and skills of all players regardless of their competence levels. Although most of the tips do assume some knowledge of counting, novices and expert counters alike can benefit from the assorted advice, which is presented here in no particular order.

1. Follow these two playing rules alone, to reduce the house edge in blackjack to approximately 1%: (i) Stand when you hold 12–16 versus dealer stiff up-cards. (ii) Hit your 12–16 when dealer shows pat up-cards.

2. When you decide to play shoe games, look for a dealer who places the plastic shuffle card the deepest, i.e., as close as possible to the last card that could possibly be dealt. Dealers have some discretion about where this reminder is inserted, and since they hate to shuffle they will sometimes stick it less than one deck from the bottom. This practice increases your profits when the TC is up, especially toward the end of every shoe.

3. Blackjack is a mini-war between you and the casino. Only if you take all of the little battles seriously will you emerge victorious in the end. Therefore, adopting a quasi-spy demeanor and mentality is almost a necessity. Try to be unobtrusive, quiet, and polite, like the "average" tourist, but keep your mission in mind. You are there to make money.

4. Keep a secret written record of all your playing results—not only how much you win or lose per session but also where you played, how long you were there, rule variations encountered, and even specific dealers and pit personnel present. This way you can avoid suspicion by not returning too soon to casinos that may have noticed you, especially during the same personnel shift.

5. Although the temptation is great, resist the free alcoholic beverages that are offered at most casinos while you are playing. The main reason is that you will make mistakes in your play directly proportional to the amount of liquor you consume. Also, you may draw attention to yourself if you order a drink and then have to leave the table before it arrives because the TC has dropped drastically.

6. Playing with a partner or two that you can trust can be beneficial for all concerned. Not only can you count at different tables in uncrowded casinos and secretly signal each other whenever conditions may warrant, but by combining your bankrolls you can more easily range your bets in accordance with the Kelly Criterion without violating the 2% Rule. Partnerships also diffuse the risk that any of you will experience Gambler's Ruin, especially if all members of the team can play competently.

7. By playing two hands of $5 each, instead of one hand of $10, you reduce your risk without changing your expected win-rate. With multiple hands, you can get twice the money on the table under favorable conditions without obviously ranging your bets at all. Some casinos require at least double-the-minimum bets on multiple hands, to protect themselves against this practice. However, if you're at a $2 table and the TC warrants a $10 bet, you are further ahead to play two spots of $5 each—another reason to choose uncrowded tables.

8. While playing, try to become completely detached emotionally and financially from the size of your bet and from whether you happen to be winning or losing at the time. Feeling elated over how much you are up, or too concerned about being down a few dollars, can distract you from efficient playing. Evaluating your situation during the shuffle is preferable and is perfectly acceptable.

9. It's worth dropping in to the Gambler's Book Club, a bookstore located at 630 South 11th Street in Las Vegas, if you are in that vicinity. This store carries all the latest blackjack newsletters, books, and

information that you could ever need. The owner, Mrs. Edna Luckman, has shown me around personally, and her staff is just as friendly and helpful as she is.

10. At the beginning of a shoe, be somewhat wary in your wagering, and range your bets slightly more conservatively. An early TC in shoe games is not quite as "true" as it sometimes appears. The closer you get to the end of the shoe, the more accurate and reliable it becomes.

11. Whether or not to surrender, when permitted, should always be considered your highest priority play. In other words, proceed to split, hit, or stand only if your hand is not to be surrendered, or if surrendering is not allowed.

12. Other factors being equal, choose a table that has a young, female dealer. Studies have shown that players actually do win more from such dealers.

13. When learning BS or MBS, it is better to use the practice exercises presented in this book rather than dealing out actual hands to yourself from a deck of cards. Although the latter more closely represents the casino experience, you may not receive all of the important beginning two-card possibilites in such "real" practice sessions. It could take you thousands of hands before every possible combination was dealt randomly. Stick to the printed exercises until you have mastered them completely, then proceed to the more concrete.

14. Although it is a player's prerogative to ask for a shuffle after any hand, you should never exercise this right. Normal players (and dealers alike) hate shuffling, because it is boring and slows down the action of the game. If the TC goes extremely sour, consider asking to be dealt out of the next hand—if the pit boss isn't nearby or apt to observe you. Then, if the count stays just as low or goes even worse, you can ask the dealer for a marker while you "visit the restroom." Of course, you will coincidentally arrive back during a shuffle! If you've already used the washroom excuse with that dealer, maybe it's time you left that table in order "to get something to eat."

15. Whenever the rules are the same, always choose a table that allows the lowest betting limit. You will certainly attract less attention there than if you were to play at a $100 minimum table. Low-limit tables tend to be more crowded, but there is also less chance that the dealer there will be a cheat. Pit bosses put their most experienced dealers at

the higher-limit tables. With lower minimums you will lose less during negative counts.

16. Although most casinos these days are completely honest, some are not. Be aware that the dealer may be cheating you or other players, for a variety of reasons. If you suspect a dishonest dealer, leave the table as quickly and quietly as possible. You have nothing to gain from a confrontation.

17. Some casinos use no shuffle cards in double-deck games. It is left entirely to the discretion of the dealer, when there is less than a deck left, whether or not to deal another hand before shuffling. When the count is positive and the cards are running low, this is often a good time to place a small bet (the table minimum is sufficient) for the dealer, since he is then more likely to deal one more round, rather than shuffling-up immediately. Tips are very important to dealers, since they make an amount equivalent to their wages from them. You not only create favor for yourself with the dealer by this gesture, you may both come up winners on these "extra" hands.

18. Play only with your "head," never your "heart." Follow the BS or MBS consistently, and do not let intuition or hunches dictate any of your decisions. If negative emotions arise, it's time to push away from the table. This usually happens when you are mentally fatigued or in the midst of a losing streak. The temptation is to abandon your game plan and win everything back with one big wager. Don't try it. Instead of penalizing yourself that way, this is an excellent opportunity to take a time-out.

19. The ideal situation, of course, is to have a table all to yourself. Although this is a matter of prestige for some high rollers, it is not recommended for beginning players. One-on-one with the dealer can be intimidating. The dealer will often talk to you too much, thereby disturbing your counting calculations, or will try to pressure you into playing faster than you would normally like to do. Neither of these situations is conducive to profitable blackjack. But once you learn how to take control and pace such a "private" game to your own ideal speed, there are larger profits to be had in these head-to-head sessions.

First of all, there is no chance of your missing cards, since they are all either yours or the dealer's. When the count goes up, *only* you profit, since you don't have to share the good cards with other players. In any given time period, you can get in five or six times the number of hands you could normally play at a full table. In short, you can enjoy all the advantages playing solo, while suffering no disadvantages.

20. Try to make a habit of continually hiding away chips, especially when you're ahead. Palm away your winnings a few at a time whenever nobody is watching. If you can't manage to pocket them secretly while sitting at the table (during a shuffle, for instance), do it when you're in the washroom or walking between tables. Make absolutely certain that no one detects this practice, since it will work against you if you are spotted. "Ordinary" players tend to revel in their winnings and would never try to hide them. Only a counter would do something like that. Do it, though, because pit bosses always notice when players start to accumulate piles of chips. By constantly needing to buy more chips, you'll be viewed as just another loser and no threat to the establishment. Furthermore, any "eccentric" plays you may make will tend to be more tolerated, and you'll be allowed to proceed with your game plan largely unmolested by floor personnel.

21. Coloring up chips at the table is never a good idea. You only draw attention to yourself and allow the dealers and pit bosses to see more easily how much you've won. Besides, it looks suspicious to be coloring up to greens or blacks when all you normally bet are reds. The average player simply wouldn't do it. A better practice is to wait until your pockets start to bulge, then casually proceed indirectly to the cashier's cage to cash them out.

22. Some "superstitious" players don't like to play the first hand after a shuffle, especially in single- or double-deck games. They prefer to sit and count the cards for the first round. Their reasoning is that it is easiest for a dealer to cheat (especially the player at first base) right after shuffling-up. There is little need for you to adopt this habit, however, since as soon as you suspect the dealer may be a cheat, you should be out of there. There are too many honest games around to chance playing with a crooked dealer. Besides, sitting out hands always draws attention to yourself.

23. When counting Aces on the side, count backward, thereby saving the subtraction step. That is, in a double-deck game, when you see the first Ace say "7" to yourself, then "6" as you see another, and so on. You always know exactly how many are available to be dealt. This is also an

easier way to keep track of 5s, for those players who may wish to use Thorp's Five-count strategy.

24. When you have a wide choice of casinos, as in Atlantic City or Las Vegas, it is best to play less than two hours in any one, per personnel shift. Even this length of time should be spent at several different tables. This is advisable for two reasons: First of all, floor people tend to notice winners, although the amounts won may be truly insignificant. You will stand out less when you move from table to table, possibly through several different pits. Second, you always do better when mentally and physically fresh. Planted in the same spot too long, you get too comfortable and are apt to lose your concentration more easily or get careless.

25. Flat betting while following proper MBS will never tip you off as a counter. Few pit bosses actually know correct BS, let alone its modifications. Even fewer are familiar with any counting systems. They do know, however, that counters generally vary the size of their bets as the composition of the remaining cards changes. Flat bettors are never barred from any casino.

26. If your last bet was large (five or six units), and the shoe runs out, you are often wiser to leave the table during the shuffle, rather than stay on and start the new shoe with a single-unit bet again. The reason is simple: Unless you were a counter, why would you reduce your bet so drastically just because the dealer shuffled? It's a dead giveaway if you do. Dealers and floor people are trained to pick up on such practices. Leaving the table at shuffle time, however, is a common occurrence that goes unnoticed. Many regular gamblers use this time for a break. How crowded the casino is, of course, should partly influence your decision to try another table in this situation. If you cannot readily play elsewhere, reducing your opening bet to, say, three units might be an acceptable alternative, especially if you believe the pit boss may be aware of the size of your last wager.

27. This one is a corollary to tip 26. Never pull back a large bet and replace it with the minimum simply because the dealer is going to shuffle. This situation happens more frequently in single- and double-deck games when you may already have placed your bet for the upcoming hand. Leaving the table is neither reasonable nor practical in these situations. This dilemma will ocur less frequently if you cultivate

the habit of generally being the last player to push out a wager before every hand.

28. Never stack up your winnings in orderly piles. This habit only allows casino personnel to more easily count their losses. Also, regularly bet with mixed-denomination chips. A quarter (green) with a couple of nickels (reds) or silver on top are less noticeable than a tall stack of reds. Dealers and floor people will tend to be more occupied with determining your correct payoffs than with the overall amounts won on such hands.

29. When tracking cards, train yourself to think of the count as being "up" or "down" rather than plus/minus or positive/negative. For example, " $-1$ " is easier and quicker to verbalize mentally as "down 1," as opposed to "negative 1" or "minus 1." Saying the number to yourself in a deeper tone of voice is also an effective way of distinguishing between "down" and "up" integers. Better still, "plus" counts should be thought of as ordinary whole numbers, (e.g., " $+7$ " as just plain "7"), with no positive- or plus-sign whatsoever attached. Only the negative integers need their minus-sign designation. This habit will save you time, effort, and possible confusion when counting, especially until you gain more experience.

30. "Sitting out" or "passing" hands only draws unnecessary attention to yourself immediately as a possible counter. An ordinary player wouldn't do this; he's there to gamble, not just to sit and watch. Be prepared to leave the table if your pass is questioned. Make sure the count is poor enough to justify your exit from the game, since some casinos have no-midshoe-entry policies which require players to wait until after a shuffle to re-enter.

31. Don't always make your playing decisions as fast as you can. The average player has to think a little before hitting a soft 18 against the dealer's 9, etc. By emulating the usual loser's slower playing style, you are less likely to be seen as a winner, barred, noticed as a counter, or even tagged as a "correct" player.

32. Never advise another player at your table about anything. Even if someone asks you directly about whether to hit, stand, double, split, surrender, take insurance, or any other information, just plead ignorance. Say, "It's your money; you have to make the decisions! If you want to give it to me, then I'll play with it my way." There are at least

five good reasons for refraining from this otherwise ego-building practice: (i) You will never be rewarded in any tangible way if the player takes your advice and wins, but you certainly will be blamed if he loses. (ii) You don't need the "expert" label drawing unnecessary attention to yourself from both dealers and pit bosses alike. (iii) Teaching others how to play correctly slows down the game for everyone at the table; you usually end up answering "why" questions, then arguing about the merits of various plays with some other well-intentioned player. (iv) Good advice is seldom truly appreciated. Most players are there merely to have a little fun. If they really wanted to know how to play the game, they would have bought a book like this and learned beforehand. Whether or not they win or lose a few dollars is usually irrelevant. Their primary purpose at the table is almost certainly not to learn how to play blackjack properly. (v) Playing the Good Samaritan will eventually interfere with your own card-counting calculations and result in financial losses to yourself. Someone will inevitably ask you a question just at a critical point in your own decision-making process, which will interfere with optimum play on your part.

33. Unless you plan to ask for comps later, always buy chips in small transactions, i.e., $50 worth or less at a time. You will avoid extra attention this way and appear more like an average small-time player. At a low-limit table especially, it looks very suspicious when someone buys in with a $100 bill or more, then proceeds to wager only $1 or $2 per hand.

34. You've probably heard the old adage, "Never leave the table while you are winning!" Regardless of how poor the playing conditions may become, it is obviously smart to play as long as you're making money. Unfortunately, many people interpret this saying as meaning you should only leave a loser. Keep playing until you begin to lose. No matter how much money you have made in the session, once you reach your stop-loss limit as described in chapter 5, walk away.

35. Cultivate an "act" of some kind to divert suspicion away from the fact that you are a threat to the casino. A tired tourist who can't add very quickly, perhaps just learning the game, is a suitable disguise that is easy to maintain convincingly. In many cases, it is essential that you maintain an act in order to avoid getting barred. You must keep in mind primarily why you are there—to win money steadily and undetected, over short periods of time. You won't be able to do this if you aren't allowed to play.

36. One way to win without actually learning to count the cards yourself is to find a counter and carefully mimic his bet-ranging. Play your hands according to BS. Proper ranging with BS is more successful than flat betting while playing MBS correctly, according to Griffin's *Theory of Blackjack.* Besides, only rarely is MBS required anyway. The main thing is to get more money out onto the table when the count is good and you have the advantage.

37. If you wish to be very conservative and take 99% of the gamble out of the game, play *only* where the count is positive. This is referred to as "Wonging," since Stanford Wong was the first to openly advocate such a practice. Make your way slowly around the pit, sliding in bets whenever you see positive situations. Continue playing at a table until the count goes negative, then move on. You don't get in as many hands with this style of play, and you tend to draw attention to yourself, but the pit personnel will normally not bother you as long as your wagers are small. By playing only when you have the advantage, you will usually make money every session. One disadvantage of this type of play is that you tend to get tired of standing unless you are in excellent physical condition. You will rarely find situations where the counts remain positive long enough for you to sit down at any table for more than a few hands at a time.

38. Don't socialize at the tables. Be pleasant in manner, but speak only when necessary. Remember, you are there to make money, not friends. The last thing you need is a player or dealer barking gregariously in your ear while you're trying to decide how best to range your next bet according to some obscure MBS play that you can barely recall.

39. Never ask to see the card that the dealer burns after a shuffle. Although it certainly would assist in determining the correct TC, only a counter would be interested in seeing it. No need to possibly arouse such suspicion over a single unseen card.

40. If you notice a pit boss observing you carefully while flipping through a pile of photos, it's time to move on to another casino. Don't wait to get barred. You can always drop back there later when the shift changes.

41. Maintaining an accurate Hi-Low RC can sometimes be a chore for beginners. One way to ease this constant pressure is to mentally "cancel" high and low cards that appear together or in the same group,

without actually including them into the count at all. For example, count the following groups of exposed cards for yourself:

$$2, 5, 7, A, T \quad 3, 9, T \quad 4, T, 2, A \quad 3, T, 8$$

Instead of counting them individually, you may have noticed that each group's total is zero. In the first case, the 2 and 5 cancel the A and T; similarly with the others. As you view such situations there is often no need to update your RC whatsoever. With a little practice using this method, it is possible to determine an overall table count quite effortlessly from little more than a glance. This skill is particularly useful if you are at a full table and using merely plus-count wagering (explained in chapter 6), or when the dealer flips over a blackjack and immediately starts scooping up the cards before you have begun counting them.

42. Do not play any game where the rules are too restrictive. If the place is too crowded or other playing conditions are not suitable, try another casino and come back to this one at some later time. If you have no alternative casino available, then you may decide to play a few hands very selectively and conservatively, i.e., only when the TC reaches 3 or more. Remember, you are there to win; therefore, it makes no sense to hand over your chips arbitrarily and needlessly if you know the odds are against you. I remember visiting the Casino de Montreal a few years ago and walking out without playing a single hand: The place was packed, and the rules were attrocious.

43. Hesitating unduly before putting your bet out is an indication that you may be a counter. Try never to seem indecisive about the size that your next wager should be. Only counters would be concerned about proper-sized bets.

44. By playing more small-stake hands when you have an advantage, you vastly increase your chances of doubling your bankroll, rather than playing fewer hands of larger wagers each. (See "Calculating Appropriate Bet Sizes," chapter 4.)

45. Never increase your bet merely to catch up after a big loss or losing streak. This practice is sometimes called "chasing your losses," and although it is tempting to do, it can be disastrous. If you continue to lose, it could completely destroy your chances of breaking even during the session. You don't need to run the risk of being totally discouraged

as a result of an even bigger loss. Remember that the only justification for increasing the size of your last wager is a more favorable TC.

46. Some casinos require all wagers to be made in even-dollar increments, to avoid problems in paying off blackjacks. Where $2.50 chips are permitted to be wagered, payoff policies differ from one casino to another. Some round up blackjack payoffs, always giving $4.00 for the $2.50 chip. In the places that round off to the nearest dollar, you can take advantage of this bit of "bonus" money by making your bets total odd-dollar increments, e.g., $3.50, $5.50, etc., in order to benefit from the round-off. While not worth the trouble for most players, it is nevertheless a valid consideration.

47. If you happen to lose your entire playing stake during a session, physically remove yourself from the casino immediately. Wallowing in your depression serves no useful function and may lead to rash acts that could actually increase your losses. Walking back to your hotel room will provide the necessary cooling-off period in which you can more objectively evaluate why you lost. Perhaps you should not have been in that casino in the first place, because of its poor playing conditions. Maybe you should have been playing more conservatively. Without becoming paranoid, ask yourself: Could the dealer have been cheating?

As long as you were following your game plan and playing correctly, there is no need to take a beating personally. Perhaps your losses were merely a result of an extended stretch of stiff hands and unlucky hits. Try to calmly accept the fact that these things happen to everyone from time to time. Probability theory and MBS don't guarantee that you always win, just that you mostly do whenever you play with the odds in your favor. In any case, use this down-time constructively to update your game plan for future sessions.

48. Don't feel guilty about playing smart and winning. The chips you win represent your money, no longer the casino's—even though their name is still on them. Skill alone has provided you with your advantage. The casinos grab every chip that they possibly can; everyone from hopeless drunks to beginning players who don't even know enough to double on 11s are their hapless victims. No need to show pity for the poor, innocent casinos by giving their money back.

49. If you notice the dealer paying off a push or overpaying a blackjack, you might decide to point it out if it's for your own hand; otherwise keep

quiet. Other players may resent your imposing your own morality upon them. An honest dealer will collect just as much money accidentally as he pays out, so it all balances in the end. And some dealers even take offense when improper payouts are pointed out to them. If "mistakes" start to happen too frequently, you are wiser to change tables. You don't need the extra mental stress of having to check up on the dealer's payoffs every hand or worrying that the dealer might be a cheat.

50. If you notice a dealer shuffling-up on you every time you raise your bets, especially in a single- or double-deck game, you can sometimes turn the tables on him. The casinos often instruct their dealers to shuffle whenever a bigger wager is placed suddenly, since they are hoping to thereby eliminate any advantage a counter may possess. This is known as "preferential" shuffling. When this happens you can be fairly certain that you have been "made," and the dealer is trying to shuffle away any positive count that may have arisen, by dealing the next hand from a neutral deck or shoe. So, if you have the nerve and financial freedom, try this for fun:

When the TC goes negative, shove out a much larger wager instead of leaving the table. The dealer may then proceed to shuffle away the disadvantage for you. Pull back a chip or two during the shuffle, just as an inexperienced counter would do. Then proceed to keep your "neutral" bets flat, but slightly higher than normal, whenever the TC is positive. This trick works only if the dealer is consistent (and you are not asked to leave the casino), but if it does succeed you may never have to play during a poor TC at that table again.

51. Never bad-mouth a dealer about poor cards you may receive. Honest dealers have no control over which cards come out at any particular time. There is no point in alienating dealers; in fact, there are good reasons to keep them on your side. If a dealer likes you, he may overlook the fact that you could very well be a counter, and consequently may not signal a floor person to turn up the heat.

52. There is no need to continue counting once you see the shuffle card come out. This is especially true if you are at first base and have finished playing out your hand, or anywhere at the table and are sitting with a pat total. Take this opportunity to casually gaze around the casino, or just relax. It's important not always to seem interested in precisely which cards other players get.

53. As your blackjack "vacation" nears an end, you can afford to be less diligent in your "act" to avoid being barred. After all, you will likely not be excluded from all the casinos during your last day or two, no matter how blatantly obvious your counting becomes. Being less paranoid will also enable you to range your bets more aggressively and you can concentrate upon playing under these optimum conditions only.

54. If you are ever asked by floor personnel to leave a casino, do so without a fuss. You might innocently ask, "What did I do wrong?" but don't make a scene. If you leave quietly you will no doubt be able to return unnoticed during the next shift, but if you create a lasting unfavorable impression as a know-it-all card-casing wiseguy you can kiss your future anonymity there goodbye.

55. Do not hesitate to double soft 19s or soft 20s versus 5s or 6s whenever the TC is greater than 5, despite the often near-violent protestations that will inevitably ensue. Well-intentioned dealers and fellow players alike will try their best to save you from these "foolish" plays. When you insist upon holding your course, watch them wag their heads and smile piteously. After the dealer busts, however, try to ignore their comments about how lucky you were. In one sense, they will be right: The "luckiest" players are, indeed, the ones who know the most about the game and play it according to correct MBS.

56. When the TC goes very positive, feel free to range your bets somewhat wider when playing shoe games, since the dealer will rarely employ a preferential shuffle until the plastic shuffle card actually appears. You may be risking a little heat from the floor, but it could be well worth it. An unusually large bet placed abruptly during a single- or double-deck game more easily prompts a shuffle, since the cards are held in the dealer's hands and shuffling is more of an arbitrary decision.

57. Be a patient winner rather than a hasty loser. Keep in mind that the normal win-rate for the dealer is 47% of total hands played, while the player's win-rate is only 43%—even under favorable playing conditions. Pushes will occur approximately 10% of the time (see Silberstang's *Winning Blackjack for the Serious Player*, page 141). Although you should always expect to lose more hands than you win, you make money because of the options available to you that the dealer cannot exercise. You can double, split, or take insurance when the odds are in your favor. You can surrender, too, and only lose half your bet.

And don't forget about blackjacks giving you 3-to-2 payoffs; therefore, unlike the dealer you make an extra half-bet on all such naturals. *You can always get more money out on the table whenever you have the advantage.* Ironically, by losing more hands than you win, you can still end up ahead even without counting the cards, simply by playing BS correctly and biding your time.

58. When using the traditional Hi-Low counting system, remember that your TC is not completely reliable for making insurance decisions. In a single-deck game, for example, an RC of 4 can produce a TC of 13 or more. This could be very misleading, since the remaining cards might *all* be non-T's! Although unlikely to occur, such a situation would obviously result in improper insurance-taking advice. This is a weakness in the Hi-Low system, so you need to place insurance bets somewhat conservatively. To be absolutely certain of making proper insurance wagers, you need to keep an Ace side-count and be prepared to adjust the TC accordingly or learn to implement Thorp's Ten-count strategy flawlessly.

59. If it takes you hours getting to and from the casino which has the best playing conditions—e.g., the Vegas Club in downtown Las Vegas from the Luxor, which is high on the Strip—your playing time there will be obviously reduced, and you may not be as mentally sharp while you are there. A casino that has slightly less liberal rules but is closer to your hotel room is usually the smarter choice overall.

60. Flat betting even though you are playing proper MBS will not win you more money in the long run than merely correct bet-ranging played according to ordinary BS, unless you are Wonging or being very conservative and playing, for example, with a TC of only +3 or more.

61. Doubling 11 vs A is a good idea in single-deck games, especially if your hand consists of 5,6 instead of, say, 9,2. The 5 and 6 are both cards that you do not want remaining in the deck, because they would hurt you on a double-down. The 9 in your hand is a card that could be able to help you almost as much as a T, so chances of a good double are reduced when you are already holding a 9.

62. "What you don't know can't hurt you," the old saw goes. In blackjack, however, it's precisely what you don't know that hurts you the most! Only by playing optimally can you obtain the greatest advantage. Being a skilled counter and being knowledgeable about proper MBS plays is the only sure path to definitive playing and winning.

63. Never more than double the size of your last bet. No matter what the count soars to, it is too risky to draw undue attention to yourself by ranging your wagers up too drastically.

64. According to Lawrence Revere's *Playing Blackjack As a Business*, page 118, you are better off simply playing perfect BS than using any count system if you are occasionally making playing errors. In other words, if you're planning on beating the casino game, you have to make the effort to follow the rules and do it right. Misplaying one hand in twenty is enough to eliminate any player's edge.

65. To virtually remove all risk from the game, the prerequisites for the nongambler are:

a. Count perfectly.
b. Range bets correctly.
c. Implement MBS flawlessly.
d. Never play negative TC's.
e. Guess at nothing.

66. In games that are dealt down, don't make any effort to hide your cards. It can't possibly help you in any way, and it only hurts other counters when you treat your hands as if you were playing poker.

67. Overbetting is the easiest road to failure. Never do it, even though it is often tempting. You overbet when you (a) play at tables with minimums that are too high (your minimum bet should be no more than 5% of your session stake), (b) overestimate your advantage, and therefore your bet is not appropriately related to your chances of winning according to the Kelly Criterion, or (c) bet more than 2% of your total bankroll on any one hand (no matter how high the TC), a practice that can quickly lead to gambler's ruin.

68. Although luck is always a factor in winning, remember that it is skill alone that will allow you to prevail in the long run. Luck is fickle; that you will win adhering to MBS plays is a fact. Avoid the temptation of becoming a VIP—Viscerally Influenced Player.

69. Do not walk around with a large roll of $100 bills, even if you are a big player. Skilled pickpockets abound who can relieve you of the whole wad without your slightest suspicion or knowledge. All casinos provide free-of-charge lines of credit from which you can draw playing markers for whatever amount you wish.

70. Avoid playing with "shills" whenever possible. A shill is a player hired by the casino primarily to attract customers to the table, to perpetuate poor playing habits, or to interfere with counters. Since they play with only house money, they consequently never tip the dealers. Shills never double or split, but they always take insurance. They often stand on all soft totals, and sometimes even stiff totals versus the dealer's pat up-cards. Splitting T's (and even 5s) is a common practice for shills, and they will often surrender perfectly good hands for no apparent reason. (They are often viewed as merely "inexperienced" players, which may explain where the superstition about not playing with beginners originated.) Shills can be used to disrupt the concentration of suspected counters—one of the many forms of "heat" that can be arbitrarily applied by casino personnel. A shill must leave the table if requested by a legitimate player, but simply finding another table for yourself is more advisable since only a counter would care.

71. Learn to look relaxed and happy while you play, even though your brain may be racing. If the casino personnel finger you as a counter, you may not live to fight another day (metaphorically speaking, of course).

72. The following levels of play illustrate the recommended stages through which all blackjack players should ascend as they move from beginner to expert. The beauty of the progession lies in the fact that the skills are cumulative; each succeeding level builds upon the one before.

Level 1: Play BS (perhaps imperfectly) while flat betting the lowest table minimums available.

Level 2: Implement a side-count of As, 5s, or preferably the Hi-Low plus-count wagering (see chapter 6), while maintaining correct BS plays.

Level 3: Use the Hi-Low RC bet-ranging guide (see chapter 6) and play your hands according to BS.

Level 4: Incorporate sound money management advice with appropriate Hi-Low TC wagering and continue adhering to 100% correct BS plays.

Level 5: After proper Hi-Low TC wagering, use MBS-2 integers (see chapter 7) in order to play most hands optimally.

Level 6: Utilize advanced Hi-Low MBS-4 and MBS-5 indices to

govern all plays after placing correct TC wagers; an Ace side-count is necessary to make informed insurance decisions.

Level 7: Follow all of the playing advice offered within this text, and learn to implement a more efficient counting system, which necessarily includes various side-counts. (Note: This is a truly professional level, which cannot be achieved by most players. Systems more powerful than Hi-Low necessarily sacrifice simplicity for minute financial gains.)

73. Where shuffling machines are not in use, it is sometimes possible to track "clumps" of high or low cards through the shuffling process and gain an advantage during the next shoe by knowing roughly where to expect them. Being the player allowed to cut with the shuffle card is a big advantage when using this method.

74. Playing during off-hours can usually improve your chances of finding favorable conditions. From 4:00 to 10:00 A.M. and from 4:00 to 6:00 P.M., most tables are less crowded, thereby allowing you more hands per session and possibly some unmolested one-on-one play.

75. Wherever dealers are still required to peek at their hole cards, a "double-take" when they have a T showing can often be an advantage. Since small cards more closely resemble Aces, dealers sometimes have to look twice or extra carefully to be sure they do not have blackjacks. If you notice such a double-peek or unusual inspection you may be wise to stand with all your stiff totals and double on all 10s and 11s under these circumstances. The dealer will likely have to draw an additional card and end up busting.

76. Simply by placing a few small bets for the dealer after big payoffs or blackjacks, you can easily ingratiate yourself. I have had friendly "toked" dealers begin showing me the burn cards without being asked. On more than one occasion, when they were showing T's as their up-cards, I have had such dealers routinely skip quickly past my stiff totals to the next player. The first time this happened, I objected, since I had obviously planned to take a hit. "Do you really want another card?" a cute little Asian dealer asked with a twinkle in her eye. I caught myself just in time, remembering that she had already peeked at her hole card. Sure enough, she flipped over a 6 and proceeded to bust. When you are winning and are sharing the wealth a little, the dealers want you to keep

on winning and playing at their table. Unfortunately, some players are as tight as bark to the proverbial tree, and suffer because of it.

77. To achieve the maximum advantage from counting, range your bets as widely as the table limits allow—within your 2% guideline. A ten-unit spread is generally acceptable, although an even greater range is theoretically better. With a great enough spread you never need to ask to be dealt out of any game because of poor counts, for you will have an insignificant sum wagered; however, when the TC's are very positive you stand to make the big bucks.

78. Don't always begin each shoe with minimum wagers. This is a practice beginning counters ideally follow, and it will label you as such immediately. Occasionally start with a bet of one-third your maximum wager and adjust it up or down from there as the TC develops.

79. Try not to play at any one table for more than an hour, especially if you are winning. Bosses are paid to notice when the dealers' chip trays are being depleted, and you will likely be marked as a winner even though you may be hiding chips successfully. If you change tables or pits continuously, your play is more apt to go unnoticed.

80. Never complain about anything, except perhaps an incorrect payoff to yourself. If necessary, do this quietly and politely, and if it happens more than once, move to another dealer.

81. In tournament (or mini-tournament) play, remember that luck, money management, and playing skill determine the winners—in exactly that order. Even if you are fortunate enough to win a mini-tournament, your "fifteen minutes of fame" may be sufficient to bring your face to the attention of casino personnel and destroy any future anonymity there.

82. Listen to, but don't heed, dealers' advice on how to play your hand. If they really knew how to play the game, they would be on the other side of the table making a lot more than minimum wage plus tips.

83. Whenever you have ambiguous playing options such as whether to split or double, the best decision may not always be clear from MBS tables. If surrender is not an option, the highest priority is usually given to splitting over doubling. Using the 4,4 versus 6 as an example, the index for doubling the 8 is 2, but the index for splitting the pair is −2. Therefore, when the TC is −2 or more, split the 4s instead of doubling your 8. The obvious exception is a pair of 5s. When not surrendering or

splitting 8s or 7s, stand with your 16s and hit your 14s on any positive count.

84. Do not play Spanish 21. In chapter 2 this game was described as the most reprehensible variation of blackjack that is currently offered to unsuspecting players. Its rules are much more liberal than those of normal blackjack, and it offers many special bonuses as well. So why is this blackjack look-alike so deadly? As the proverbial gypsy maintains, "The answer is in the cards!" Unbeknownst to most players of Spanish 21, all the 10s have been removed from the shoe! From chapter 6 it is obvious how important big cards are to the player. Therefore, beginning each shoe with a TC of $-4$ represents insurmountable odds.

85. After being away from the game for a month or so, you will likely be rustier than you may realize. Review MBS charts and practice counting before your return to casino action. Even if you normally play at $25 tables, break yourself in at the lowest-minimum tables available for your first session, or until you are sure that you are up to speed once more.

86. Where "multiple-action" games are offered (described in chapter 2), a little back-counting (Wonging) can be a boon for counters. Since this game looks odd, it is only natural for regular blackjack players to observe a few rounds before sitting down. When the count is high, by playing the three first-base positions you are virtually assured of drawing beneficial cards even at a full table.

87. Always try to chose single- or double-deck games over shoe games if the rules are similar. Although it is easier for the dealer to cheat when cards are held in the hand, these games are easier to track accurately. Beginning counters find it simpler to estimate the TC when playing with only one or two decks. And, if you lose track of the count completely, you won't have to wait as long for the next shuffle in order to start another RC. Even an experienced counter can find himself scrambling to tally up Hi-Low point totals when a shoe-dealer flips over a blackjack at a full table and immediately begins scooping up the bets and cards with both hands. You are also more likely to get much higher TC's in these games than with shoes.

88. Make sure that you don't stand out in any way while in a casino. Wearing expensive jewelery or clothing just draws attention to yourself, and you are not there to impress anyone. To remain inconspicuous you

need to look like the average loser; otherwise, you will be seen as a winner and will be more apt to end up getting barred from play.

89. If you cannot remember precisely a specific MBS integer that you need, it is better to guess at it than to play BS alone. After all, MBS plays are never exact at the best of times, since all TC's are only estimates themselves. However, never modify a BS play without very good MBS reasoning to justify it.

90. As a counter, you will generally have your biggest wagers out near the end of a shoe, but you can never be sure exactly when the dealer will be forced to shuffle if the shuffle card is not visible. When the shuffle does come, in order to disguise the necessary reduction in your bet you could possibly play two spots for the first round, if the table isn't crowded. This not only discourages passing players from joining the game during a shuffle (since fewer boxes will appear to be open), but it will actually increase your odds of winning on a neutral deck.

Spreading less than half your last large bet into two adjacent boxes makes it less obvious that you have drastically cut back your wager. Otherwise, you are wiser to proceed with a fairly large single bet on the freshly shuffled neutral shoe, at least occasionally, and especially if the pit boss is observing your play at all. Similarly, be careful not to reduce your bet too much between hands just because the count goes cold. Gradual changes in all bet-ranging is the key. It can avoid getting you identified as a counter and subsequently removed from the game.

91. Avoid single-deck games that employ "high" dealers. A dealer using an awkward close-to-the-chest style of delivery could be a cheat. It is easier for crooked dealers to go completely undetected when dealing "seconds" by holding the deck at about the players' eye level.

92. Utilizing the information contained in this text, you will not actually be gambling when you play blackjack. Rather, you may think of the game as an investment opportunity that can provide a good rate of return on your money. Every business venture has an element of risk; few offer overall odds so firmly in your favor as skillfully played blackjack.

93. Do not be fooled into thinking that you can beat this game simply by finding a dumping table and playing there. A dumping table is one where the dealer is busting or the players are winning more than usual. Just the opposite is apt to occur if and when you join the game.

There is no reason to suspect that winning (or losing) trends will continue, unless you enjoy the advantage of the specific probabililty information available only to counters.

94. Clump tracking is a counting procedure in which you take note of bunches of high or low cards as they appear during the game and follow them through the shuffle in order to know when an advantage or disadvantage is likely to occur in the next shoe. For example, a counter notices that an extremely poor RC occurs during the first deck dealt from a shoe, say, −15. This means that the cards in the discard tray now contain fifteen more high cards than others. By paying close attention to this favorable group of cards while the dealer is shuffling at the end of the shoe, the counter knows approximately when they will appear in the following shoe. Depending upon the complexity of the shuffling pattern used, an observant player can use this information to range his bets upward at the appropriate time. If the counter gets the opportunity to cut the cards, he can often force the desired clump of cards to the front of the next shoe, and begin betting with higher than normal wagers.

Clump tracking is generally not worth the effort to learn nowadays. Although still useful on rare occasions, it is easily thwarted by casinos by utilizing a number of simple shuffling variations: (a) By using dual discard trays and alternately placing the discards into them, dealers effectively break up most clumps; any that are left are nearly impossible to follow through a shuffle. (b) If the dealer "strips" while shuffling, all but the most extreme clumps are similarly destroyed. (Stripping moves whole groups of cards from the top portion of a stack to the bottom without actually shuffling them.) (c) The "stutter-shuffle" involves the dealer taking as much as half-deck picks from stacks already shuffled once, and shuffling them with the unshuffled discards. The stuttering process is continued throughout the entire six decks, making clump tracking very difficult indeed, if not impossible. (d) The most popular method of countering clump tracking is the introduction of shuffling machines, which also speed up the game and make all types of deck stacking (the illegal practice of deliberately arranging cards in a particular order) more difficult for dealers.

95. Beginning counters are constantly losing the RC; it also happens to experienced players when they are tired or distracted. If this is a recurring problem for you, use one of your chips to physically indicate

how much the count is up (and another to show how much the count is down, if necessary) after each round of play. Turn the chip-face to correspond with the face of a clock. Since players are constantly fiddling with their chips anyway, this practice will go unnoticed.

96. Use "match-play" and other casino coupons at every opportunity. Not only do they represent free money; more important, you will resemble a typical "novice" tourist-player whenever you pull them out. After all, "a professional player would never stoop to such an undignified practice," the pit bosses think. Coupon play virtually assures anonymous heat-free playing conditions.

97. Don't be the highest roller at your table. Everyone notices the biggest bettors. Instead, if possible, find a table where someone is betting wildly and extravagantly. The size of your wagers will go completely unobserved there.

98. If you need to increase your wager, never raise it more than a unit or two while the pit boss is observing your play. With a little panache it may be possible to parlay your last win without the move seeming suspicious. ("Parlaying" is equivalent to "letting it all ride" after a win.) Playing two spots instead of one if space permits is also an acceptable method of getting twice the money on the table without drawing undue attention to the increased size of your wager.

99. Choosing low-limit tables (especially when they are not crowded) doesn't mean you will not win just as much there. You can always raise your bets in order to take advantage of high TC's when the occasions arise. They are financially safer, too; if it means that you can play more hands at low-minimum tables, you will be less likely to experience "ruin" by using many small bets rather than fewer large wagers.

100. By updating your financial position after each session, you can more properly determine your allowable bet range for future sessions. Also, watching your bankroll increase is a real comfort during those inevitable losing streaks.

101. Read this book from cover to cover again—at least once!

# Select Bibliography

Braun, Julian H. *How to Play Winning Blackjack*. Chicago: Data House Publishing, 1980.

Cardoza, Avery. *How to Win at Gambling*. New York: Cardoza Publishing, 1991.

Culbertson, Ely. *Card Games, Complete With Official Rules*. Greystone Press, 1952.

Epstein, Richard A. *The Theory of Gambling and Statistical Logic*. New York: Academic Press, 1977.

Griffin, Peter. *Theory of Blackjack: The Compleat Card Counter's Guide to the Casino Game of 21*. Lafayette, Louisiana: Huntington, 1988.

Humble, Lance, and Carl Cooper. *The World's Greatest Blackjack Book*. New York: Doubleday, 1980.

Ortiz, Darwin. *Gambling Scams*. New York: Dodd, Mead, 1984.

Patterson, Jerry L. *Blackjack: A Winner's Handbook*. New York: Perigee Books, 1990.

Revere, Lawrence. *Playing Blackjack As a Business*. New York: Lyle Stuart, 1971.

Roberts, Stanley. *The Gambling Times Guide to Blackjack*. Van Nuys, California, 1984. Carol Publishing Ed. 1990.

Silberstang, Edwin. *Winning Blackjack for the Serious Player*. New York: Cardoza Publishing, 1993.

Scarne, John. *Scarne on Cards*. New York: Crown Publishers, 1968.

Thorp, Edward O. *Beat the Dealer*. New York: Random House, 1962, 1966.

Uston, Ken, and Rapoport, Roger, *The Big Player*. New York: Holt, Rinehart & Winston, 1977.

Vinson, Barney. *Las Vegas, Behind the Tables!* Grand Rapids, Michigan: Gollehon Press, 1986 (part 1), 1988 (part 2).

Waller, Adrian. *The Gamblers*. Toronto: Clarke, Irwin, 1974.

Wong, Stanford. *Professional Blackjack*. New York: Morrow, 1981.

Wykes, Alan. *Gambling*. London: Aldus Books, 1964.

# INDEX